BEFORE ABCS AND 123S BUILDING EXECUTIVE FUNCTIONING IN CHILDREN

DISCOVER SEVEN SUPER SKILLS THAT WILL HELP KIDS UNLOCK THEIR POTENTIAL IN THE CLASSROOM AND BEYOND

A PRACTICAL GUIDE FOR PARENTS AND TEACHERS

JENNIFER STOCKREEF

Photo credit: Congerdesign

I would like to dedicate this book to my amazing family, Tom, Meg, and Anna! Their support and encouragement mean the world to me.
And also, to the incredible teachers I work with each day. I have learned so much from all of you!
Last but not least I want to thank all of my little students throughout the years and their families. You have been the inspiration for this book.

DISCLAIMER

This book about executive function is for informational purposes only and should not replace professional medical advice. Consult your physician or healthcare provider for personalized guidance. By reading this document, the reader agrees that under no circumstances is the author responsible for any losses, direct or indirect, which are incurred as a result of the use of the information contained within this document, including, but not limited to, — errors, omissions, or inaccuracies.

Please note that all effort has been expended to present accurate, up-to-date, and reliable, complete information. No warranties of any kind are declared or implied. Readers acknowledge that the author is not engaging in the rendering of legal, financial, medical, or professional advice. The content within this book has been derived from various sources.

CONTENTS

Introduction   9

1. SUPER SKILL #1: SELF-CONTROL   17
   Ben's Story   18
   Self-Control at a Glance   22
   How to Spot if a Child Is Struggling with Self-
   Control   24
   Strategies for Teaching Self-Control   29
   Be Aware of the Links Between Screen Time and
   Poor Self-Control Skills   36
   Conclusion   38

2. SUPER SKILL #2: SELF-REGULATION   41
   Ben's Story   41
   Self-Regulation at a Glance   42
   How to Spot a Child Who Is Struggling with Self-
   Regulation   46
   Strategies and Tips for Teaching Self-Regulation   48
   Games that Help Build Self-Regulation Skills   58
   Storybooks to Read to Children About Self-
   Regulation   58
   Conclusion   59

3. SUPER SKILL #3: ADAPTABLE THINKING   61
   Ben's Struggles with Adaptable Thinking   62
   Adaptable Thinking at a Glance   63
   How to Spot If a Child Is Having Trouble with
   Adaptable Thinking   64
   Strategies for Teaching Adaptable Thinking   65
   Conclusion   75

4. SUPER SKILL #4: PLANNING AND PRIORITIZING   77
   Ben's Struggles with Planning   77
   Planning at a Glance   78
   Prioritization at a Glance   79

How to Spot If a Child Is Having Trouble with
Planning and Prioritizing   80
Strategies for Developing Planning Skills in
Children   81
The Relationship between Time and Planning   83
Estimating Task Duration   84
Tips for Teaching Time Estimation   84
Tips for Allocating Time Wisely   86
The Importance of Adaptability   86
Teaching Adaptation   87
Strategies for Developing Prioritization Skills   89
The Role of Parents and Teachers   93
How Parents Can Support Planning and Prioritizing
Skills   93
How Teachers Can Support Planning and
Prioritizing Skills   96
Fun Strategy Games to Promote Planning and
Prioritizing   97
Recommended Story Book for Teaching Planning
and Prioritizing: 97
Conclusion   97

5. SUPER SKILL #5: ORGANIZATION   103
Ben's Struggles with Organization   104
Organization at a Glance   105
Benefits of Having Strong Organizational Skills   106
The Role of Problem-Solving and Resilience in
Developing Organization Skills   108
Why Organization Matters for School Learning   109
Four Ways Kids Use Organizational Skills to Learn   110
How to Spot Organizational Challenges in Children   111
Strategies for Teaching Organization   112
A Few More Thoughts on Organization   115
Children's Books about Organization That Are Fun
to Read   118
Conclusion   118

6. SUPER SKILL #6: TIME MANAGEMENT   121
Ben's Struggles with Time Management   122
Time Management at a Glance   122
The Importance of Time Management   123
Real-Life Applications   125

How to Spot If a Child Is Struggling with Time
Management   126
Strategies for Teaching Time Management Skills   127
Tips for Parents and Teachers   131
Fun Books to Read About Time Management   134
Conclusion   134

7. SUPER SKILL #7: WORKING MEMORY   137
Working Memory at a Glance   138
Examples of When We Use Working Memory   139
Why Is Working Memory Important for Children?   142
Five Ways Kids Employ Working Memory to
Enhance Classroom Learning   143
Factors Impacting the Development of Working
Memory in Children   145
How to Spot Working Memory Challenges in
Children   147
Strategies to Develop Working Memory in Children   151
Ben's Journey: Strengthening Working Memory   156
Conclusion   159

GETTING HELP AND SUPPORT FOR CHILDREN   161

Conclusion   165
Works Cited   171
References   175

INTRODUCTION

The first day of kindergarten is a significant milestone—for children and parents.

As parents, we look forward to it with an equal mixture of excitement and dread. We want our kids to excel academically and socially. We worry about how to prepare. How do we help our kids adjust? How can we ensure their success?

We know school is a steppingstone to a happy and healthy adulthood, but what about the steps in between? Why are the early years of school so important?

Kindergarten is often the first step our children take towards independence. They spend half if not all, the day away from home, socializing with peers and other adults and learning new academic skills. When we put it this way, it's obvious why early school experiences are so meaningful. There is, however, a lot more to it.

Until recently, most parents worked to prepare their children for kindergarten by teaching them beginning academic skills—how to recognize the alphabet or basic numbers. Some parents tried to be ahead of the game by focusing on reading skills—I know that was something both my mother and grandmother did to try and prepare their kids.

As a parent, I remember sitting my kids in front of *Baby Einstein* videos, hopeful that exposure to classical music and foreign languages would prepare them for academic success in the way I imagined—straight A's on report cards and early interests in diverse subjects like science and languages.

However, after teaching preschool and kindergarten for the past twenty-six years, it has become clear that academic learning is only one of the challenges for many students.

Throughout my years of teaching, I recall having many difficult conversations with parents during conferences. I would explain how their child struggled to stay focused and how hard it was for them to follow simple directions in the classroom, mostly because they found the experience of being at school so overwhelming.

It would take several more heart-to-heart conversations with these families to realize that it was more manageable for parents to focus on preparing their children for school by teaching them reading and math skills. It was much more challenging to pinpoint the underlying cause for the struggles their children were experiencing in the classroom. It was also tough for teachers to know how to help students in the classroom who were struggling with behaviors that were interfering with their ability to learn and keep pace with their classmates. Although we are becoming more familiar with executive functioning today, academic skills can still seem more important—and easier for us as parents and teachers to teach. There's also a tendency to assume that executive functioning skills come naturally or don't need to be taught. This couldn't be further from the truth. The director of the Brain and Early Experiences at Boston University, Amanda Tarullo, explains that executive functioning skills, in fact, "don't develop on their own. Instead, the relevant regions of the brain need to be activated —and often, since the brain's networks are strengthened through practice" (Tarullo, 2022b).

Many first-time parents and teachers assume that children aged four or five will stride into a kindergarten classroom with twenty other children and automatically understand that they need to listen to the teacher, follow directions, pay attention, and sit still.

It seems evident to me now, looking back, that executive functioning skills are far more critical for young children than the ability to recognize letters or numbers. As Tera Sumpter explains, "Executive Functioning is the foundation for all learning" (Tera Sumpter, 2023a).

But why exactly are executive functioning skills so necessary?

According to the Center on the Developing Child at Harvard University, executive function and the important related concept of self-regulation are "mental processes that enable us to plan, focus attention, remember instructions, and juggle multiple tasks successfully" (Center on the Developing Child, 2012).

To explain this further, they describe executive functioning skills as the air traffic control system of the brain. If you've ever been to an airport, you probably have an idea of how many planes are taking off and landing at any given time. Also, planes are moving through the sky, often along the same routes. An airport is a busy place, and the air traffic control system is vital for ensuring that every plane is safe and gets to where it needs to go. It communicates with the pilots, giving them the information they need to do their jobs efficiently and correctly. This information confirms that pilots make good decisions, can shift focus quickly if necessary, and that they do a good job.

The analogy for executive functioning works here because, just as airplanes and airport runways need air traffic control systems to keep things running smoothly, the brain also needs to have a means to filter distractions, prioritize tasks, set and achieve goals, and control impulses.

Under the umbrella of executive functioning skills, we have everything that keeps the airlines running smoothly. This means everything from problem-solving skills to emotional control. Executive functioning also affects working memory, flexible thinking, the ability to break down assignments into smaller steps, and the ability to stay on task. Planning, prioritization, and organization skills belong in this category, too. But how does this relate to learning for your child? As one authority put it, "Every social, learning, work, and living interaction requires executive function skills" (Dyslexia Inspired, 2023). Put another way, executive function skills are the bedrock for success in school and life.

Think back to when you were in school or college. Do you remember which students were the most successful? How did you manage the demands of your assignments? Chances are you remember someone from your past who was not necessarily an academic whiz but passed every class with flying colors. The closer you examine the record of people who excel in school and life, the clearer it is that the key to success is executive functioning —being organized and getting things done. Sounds pretty straightforward, doesn't it? But there is, of course, a problem.

Very few people—teachers or parents—spend time teaching executive functioning skills to kids. We might teach some of them indirectly. For example, we tell kids to sit down, stay still, and do their homework before playing. All of that counts. But we certainly don't *systematically* teach executive functioning skills. Instead, what tends to happen—as we've suggested above—is that we adults put most of the focus on academics. As parents, we worry about making sure our kids can read, write, and do basic arithmetic. Teachers, too, are under pressure to focus on things like test scores, so they also tend to concentrate on teaching academic skills.

According to Amanda Tarullo, the director of the Brain and Early Experiences Laboratory at Boston University: "When children enter kindergarten, the key question is not whether they know the alphabet or can add and subtract. Instead, the important skills should include impulse control, attention span, and emotional regulation" (Tarullo, 2022).

What Tarullo is getting at here is very much the reason for this book- "First executive function, then learning" (Sumpter, 2024b). This argument—backed up by substantial evidence—is that we all learn academic stuff much more effectively when we have executive functioning skills in place to help us. Not only that, but everyone does better *in life* when they have developed strong executive functioning skills.

According to Sumpter and experts like her, it is high time we all started shifting our focus from just teaching academic skills to also teaching executive functioning skills. Perhaps the most persuasive argument for this is that kids with strong executive functioning skills are better students—academic skills will develop easier for them. But what happens when kids don't learn executive functioning skills?

If you've ever been told that you (or perhaps your child) are unprepared, lazy, disruptive, disorganized, forgetful, distracted, or impulsive, it might well be that you're dealing with some sort of executive dysfunction. Although we don't typically teach executive functioning skills directly, we place a substantial demand on kids concerning these skills. We expect kids to master them. However, it is important to note that the part of the brain where executive function skills develop (the prefrontal cortex) does not fully mature until around the age of twenty-five. This means that even when we provide our children with explicit instruction to help them build executive function skills, it will be a work in progress.

Think about that first day of kindergarten again, but now let's do it with a focus on executive functioning. You drop your child off at school for the first time, probably in the classroom. You say goodbye and walk away. Your kid is on their own. But what do they do? First of all, they're probably in an unfamiliar environment. There are lots of kids and adults—most likely, some are strangers. There's also going to be lots of stuff. There will be toys, tables, chairs, and posters on the walls. There's lots of information —pictures, lists, charts. I know most kindergarten classrooms I've seen are laid out to be bustling, engaging environments. And you want kids to be engaged, of course. But what we're also talking about is a lot of stimulation. Without reasonable impulse control, it will be very easy for a child to become distracted almost as soon as they enter the classroom. They are probably faced with a lot of sensory input as well—loud noises, bright colors, and many objects around. Impulse control is going to have to kick in, too. Then there's the question of following instructions. Let's say the teacher asks your child to hang up their coat and put their lunchbox in their cubby before coming over and sitting down for circle time. Unlikely as it may be that an educator would expect students to do this perfectly on the first day, it's not unreasonable to assume that they will have this expectation later in the year after your child has had time to acclimate to the school routine. Even after some time getting used to things, though, the stimulus within the classroom doesn't exactly dissipate. Nor does your child necessarily develop the skills to follow multi-step directions independently. For most kids, those skills don't develop for a while, so what it looks like, when we're not looking at it with an awareness of executive functioning, is that you have a very distracted and disorganized child. They might get the first step done—taking off their coat. Maybe they manage the second step as well, putting their lunch away. But when they come to sit down for circle time, they're already looking around, reaching out for sensory input, and struggling to focus.

Let's also consider that your child will need to sit still and quietly with their peers at least some of the time in the classroom. Sitting down and paying attention will set the bar very high if they're already dealing with overstimulation and distraction because they've struggled to process multi-step directions.

Looking ahead to, let's say, middle school, we now have new demands placed on our kids. Things like time management become a challenge. We expect our middle schoolers to be able to pay attention and focus. We expect them to regulate their emotions and be able to effectively shift focus, going from one class to another without any problems. We also expect them to be able to prioritize things like homework and to remember the details of what they have to do for a given assignment. The list goes on. But suppose your child struggles with executive functioning. In that case, the demands are just piling on by this point, and you may be getting feedback that, for instance, they're too easily distracted or forget what they need to do for homework.

You get the idea.

Now, imagine, for a minute, that we have a child going into kindergarten, and they learn about executive functioning skills right away. What if parents and teachers knew to work together to help children develop executive functioning skills from day one? As parents, we could be helping our children get used to things like time management, planning, and prioritizing. We can, to an extent, model these skills for our kids, but there are also ways to teach these skills, which we will discuss in this book.

A kindergartener learning executive functioning skills, though, will be learning how to regulate their emotions, stay focused, shift tasks when necessary, follow multi-step directions, and remember details of what they're told or what they experience.

These are just some examples.

Instead of feeling upset to see their parents leave them, kids could learn to regulate their feelings of anxiety, shifting focus and letting themselves get absorbed in activities, for instance. They could also learn to use tools like checklists and reward systems to help them stay focused and transition smoothly from one task to another.

The goal of this book is to introduce you to practical strategies and activities that will help you develop executive functioning skills in children.

This book focuses on seven super skills specifically:

1. **Self-Control**
2. **Self-Regulation**
3. **Adaptable Thinking**
4. **Planning and Prioritizing**
5. **Organization**
6. **Time Management**
7. **Working Memory**

In the following chapters, we will address each one of these skills in depth, discussing why they are essential and what you can do to help develop them.

SUPER SKILL #1: SELF-CONTROL

"It is through activity that children learn to develop self-control, not through sitting still."

— *ELLEN GALLINSKI*

Imagine that you get into an argument with someone. They make you really angry. It doesn't matter whether it's something they do or say. Whatever it is, you're fuming. You can feel your fists tingling, and perhaps you're even imagining how satisfying it would be to use physical force against that person.

Now, imagine that you're playing a game of some sort with a group of people. You've been playing for a while, and your friend wants a turn. Unfortunately, though, you're super invested in what you're doing. You're in the zone! As your friend gets increasingly frustrated, what does it take for you to step away and let them have a turn?

Self-control is the magic element—and the first priority of executive functioning.

Instead of hitting the person who irritates you, you walk away and move on to something else.

You must have the self-control to step away from the game you're playing and maybe even move on to do the laundry—or any other non-preferred task.

You have to resist your impulses and inclinations, which are not skills that develop on their own.

Now, let's consider self-control as it pertains to children developing executive functioning skills.

BEN'S STORY

Ben is in sixth grade. He struggles with managing his impulses, staying organized, and getting things done. Ben is heading to meet the school bus first thing in the morning, around 7 a.m.; he frequently realizes that he's forgotten something. Some days, it's his lunch; other days, it's his change of clothes for gym class. Ben races home to grab whatever he's missing because he knows he'll get in trouble if he shows up without everything he needs for the day. Although his mom leaves a checklist by the front door detailing all that he needs on a given day, Ben runs right past it. Unfortunately, by the time he reaches the bus stop, he's too late. He missed the bus.

When he finally arrives at school, having been dropped off by his mom, Ben is already feeling very wound up. He's worried about being late for school and anxious that he might have forgotten something else. When he's at school, later in the day, the teacher asks a question about a homework assignment for the class. Ben, unfortunately, didn't manage to get his homework done either. He forgot to write the assignment in his planner and can't remember what questions he was supposed to answer. Because he doesn't want to get called on, he gets increasingly anxious and fidgets in his seat. This distracts other students and draws the teacher's attention.

By lunchtime, Ben very much needs a break, but he's so stressed out that he can't stop talking. He's speaking very loudly, and his friends are becoming annoyed by his behavior. In gym class, as everyone plays soccer, things between Ben and his friends reach a head. After being difficult at lunch, Ben is now hogging the ball in soccer, unwilling to pass to his teammates. Because he's not paying attention to what's happening on the field, he runs too close to his own goal and makes it possible for the other team to score. Ben ends the school day on bad terms with his friends, who don't want to talk to him on the way home.

Finally, still feeling wound up and on edge, Ben tries to get through his evening routine. When he's sitting in front of the television, his mother turns it off and tells him he needs to concentrate on his homework. This is the breaking point, and Ben gets really upset. He starts yelling at his mom.

His dad sends him to his room to calm down. At dinner time, he barely makes it through the meal because he is still upset with his parents. He doesn't want to talk to his mom, and he is distracted by everything around him, from his dad listening to the news to his sister talking to a friend on the phone. Getting homework done is almost impossible at this point.

By the time he gets to bed, it's well past his usual time because he's had to spend extra time working with his mom to finish his homework. Thinking about the day ahead, Ben is worried about how his friends will treat him and anxious that his mom and dad are frustrated with him. Ben feels entirely out of control and has a tough time winding down to get to sleep. Because he will be short on sleep, it's unlikely that the following day at school will be any better.

So, what does this have to do with self-control? As Tera Sumpter explains, self-control is about learning to inhibit an impulse, which itself requires several specific skills—self-awareness of the impulse, foresight of a desired outcome, and stopping before you act (Sumpter, 2024c).

In the story above, Ben lacks self-control in several instances. Most obviously, when he's sitting in class and can't stop fidgeting, when he's playing soccer with his friends and won't share the ball, and when he's at home with his mom, watching television instead of starting his homework.

In each of these situations, Ben is struggling to control his impulses. Granted, other things are going on—we'll discuss later how all the other skills are related. Along with self-control goes self-regulation and planning, for example.

Self-control is the foundation of executive functioning skills, though, for the simple reason that it feeds into everything else.

Agency is another skill worth mentioning as we discuss self-control because although having agency differs from having self-control, the two skills go hand in hand. But what is agency? Xplor Education explains, "When babies and young children grow and develop a sense of agency, they realize that they can contribute and make their own decisions and control their own lives. A sense of agency is a significant part of a strong sense of identity and has been identified as a foundation to learning and well-being" (Xplor ,2022).

Tera Sumpter connects agency and self-control by pointing out that self-control is also about giving individuals, including children, a sense that they have some choice in what's happening to them.

She writes: "Let children control their lives where and when they can. It's the only way they'll be able to practice self-direction and the development of executive functioning. Always being told what to do is external direction, not self-direction" (Tera Sumpter, 2023c). So, how can we help our kids develop agency? Here are four great ideas from Sparhawk school writer Kaitlyn MacDonald (MacDonald, 2019):

1. Give Your Child Safe Choices to Choose From

Young children can become overwhelmed by too many options. You can help your child feel agency and provide structure by organizing choices. For example, a young child can choose what outfit to wear if you give them two weather-appropriate options to choose from.

2. Help Your Child Learn from Mistakes and Allow Them to Make Them

I love this quote from Tim Elmore, *"Prepare your child for the path —Not the path for your child"* (Elmore 2014, p.197). As parents, it is hard to watch our kids struggle. We want to make their lives as easy as possible. So sometimes, even maybe subconsciously, we try to solve all their problems for them. There is even a term for this called "Bulldozer Parenting." This is where parents "bulldoze" any obstacles out of the way for their kids, so they never encounter any conflicts. The problem with this is that when they eventually have an issue, they have no way of knowing how to handle it.

Although it can be tempting to try and shield our kids from difficult situations, they will often learn best from their own mistakes. Here's an example: your child chooses to play a video game before their soccer game, and now they don't have enough time to get ready. If they arrive at the field without all of their gear, don't be too fast to swoop in and bring it to them. After learning from the consequences, calmly discuss what they could do differently next time. This will help build resiliency and ensure future success.

3. Allow Your Child to Be Responsible for Real-Life Tasks

Being accountable for something important helps build confidence. Young kids could help prepare dinner using real tools (with adult supervision), a middle school child could take care of the family pets, and a high schooler could manage and organize their weekly schedule.

4. Involve Your Kids in Goal Setting

Help your child identify their goals and support them in achieving them. For example, a five-year-old might set a goal of wanting to learn how to ride a bike without training wheels. You can support your child with this goal by helping them practice and creating a schedule for practicing.

Now, let's take a closer look at self-control.

SELF-CONTROL AT A GLANCE

According to the Understood Team, "Self-control is one of a group of skills that allows kids and adults to manage their thoughts, actions, and emotions that connect to the things that they want to do" (Griffin, 2024).

As we've suggested in the story of Ben, self-control plays a role in many basic activities—everything from sitting, waiting in line, taking turns, and interacting with others.

There are three critical areas to focus on when developing self-control: movement control, impulse control, and emotional control.

The idea of movement control is the most easily recognizable. Kids need to learn to regulate their movements to achieve self-control, so they aren't constantly moving around. Kids who can't gain movement control are often described as hyperactive, and this is typically seen as very disruptive.

On the other hand, impulse control is an even more general term, with even broader implications. Having impulse control means you aren't just going to do whatever pops into your head. Impulse control means that you can put a stop to doing something or saying something. For Ben, impulse control could mean the difference between talking non-stop with his friends all through lunch or having a meaningful conversation or two that makes him (and his friends) feel good about their relationships.

Finally, with emotional control, we have the opportunity to manage instances in which we might become upset or in which we might overreact to a given situation. Ben's interaction with his mother came down to a lack of emotional control. He didn't want the television to be turned off, so he got upset, started yelling, and lost control. Ben struggles to regulate his emotions effectively, and as a result, his feelings run wild. We've all seen it; as parents and caretakers, we often learn the signs. Kids, especially when tired, have difficulty controlling their emotions and are particularly prone to tantrums and outbursts.

But these are not the only signs of trouble with self-control.

HOW TO SPOT IF A CHILD IS STRUGGLING WITH SELF-CONTROL

Children who may need support developing self-control might demonstrate the following behaviors:

- Interrupting people in conversation
- Blurting out responses, even when not called on
- Talking non-stop
- Being overactive or restless
- Grabbing things without thinking
- Cutting in lines
- Being unable to take turns
- Getting frustrated easily
- Giving up on tasks as soon as they become challenging
- Bursting into tears quickly when upset
- Not being able to accept any kind of criticism
- Difficulty keeping their hands and feet to themselves

Now, these kinds of self-control issues have various causes. Not having self-control skills is the underlying issue with almost all of them, but we should also acknowledge the different factors.

- **Immaturity** is genuinely a reason why children lack self-control—the "kids will be kids" idea. Their brains are simply not mature yet—this is true even for teenagers. They are, in effect, still learning. There's also a pronounced difference between the capacity for impulse control when talking about a toddler versus a teenager, as you would probably expect. However, when considering the impact of maturity or immaturity, it's also worth realizing that there are developmental parameters and checks. A teenager should be much better able to control impulses than a

SUPER SKILL #1: SELF-CONTROL | 25

toddler. If you notice that your teenager cannot, for example, resist talking very loudly or taking things they shouldn't, then immaturity is not a factor.

- **Lack of sleep** is another major trigger for impulse control issues—along with a whole host of other issues. If your child has a problem with sleep and isn't getting enough of it, this could be why they are struggling with self-control. Simple strategies like enforcing an earlier bedtime or facilitating afternoon naps can help.

- **Stress and frustration** are also significant challenges for self-control. At the end of the day, it's not just "kids will be kids," but "humans will be humans." You may recognize what lack of sleep does to you—how it can make you short-tempered and unable to concentrate as you usually would. Most people feel on edge when they're tired. Your reaction times also tend to be off. Stress and frustration can have a similar effect. If you're worried about something, you're more likely to have difficulty focusing and resisting impulses. Your emotions could be all over the place, too. Impulsive behavior is much more likely to happen when you're stressed. A preoccupied mind is one considerably less likely to manage self-control. It's that simple. And it is very much the same for kids. Just like adults, kids have stresses and frustrations, too. Even very young children respond to stress. Babies react to loud, angry voices. They respond to their parents being stressed out. Toddlers and young children do this, too. When there are stressful events, kids will also tend to struggle with self-control.

Of course, not everyone reacts the same. According to clinical psychologist Dr. Matthew Rouse, "Some kids are instantaneous—they have a huge, strong reaction, and there's no lead-in or build-up. They can't inhibit that immediate behavior response." For other kids, distress will tend to build up. They will absorb a certain amount of stress and then have some kind of behavioral outburst. He explains, "You can see them going down the wrong path, but you don't know how to stop it" (Child Mind Institute and Rouse, 2024). Whether for older or younger children, the main point is learning to handle strong reactions to situations and to express emotions appropriately.

Now that we know what self-control problems look like in children, let's consider what we can do to help teach and develop self-control skills.

Although we will discuss specific strategies, let's consider some pointers by age:

- **For kids up to age two**, developing self-control is a very gradual process. There is often a dramatic gap between what infants and toddlers want and what they can do. Let's think about infants that are immobile, for example. They can't get where they want to go. They also can't feed or clean themselves, so when they experience the discomfort of being hungry or needing to be changed, they have no other option but to cry out for attention and hope that an adult will address their needs.
- **Toddlers** don't necessarily have it all that much better, either. Although they have quite a few more skills, they still don't have much control over the world around them. This is why kids often have temper tantrums—when they can't get what they want, they have an outburst.

What are some of the things you can do to help avoid a tantrum with a child under two? An excellent strategy is to provide a **distraction**. Get into the habit of distracting your infant or toddler when they are upset. For example, if your child becomes upset, try using stuffed animals or toys that play music or light up. These types of toys can be good distractions and help your little one calm down when feeling distressed.

- **For children between two and three years old**, the strategy of a time-out can be very effective. I like to use the term "take a break" instead of time-out because when trying to teach self-control, it should never feel like a punishment. Creating a designated space, like a kitchen chair or bottom stair step, will remove them from whatever stressful situation your youngster has experienced. It can help them learn the advantages of leaving a stressful situation and having time to calm down and manifest self-control. Make sure to stay with or near your child during a break. Young children need a calm adult to be with them to help regulate their feelings. You do not need to talk a lot to your child during this process. However, make sure you let them know you are there for them and that they are not alone in trying to figure out their feelings. Remember that your child is not trying to give you a hard time; they are having a hard time and need your time and attention to teach them how to cope.
- **Between the ages of three and five**, children have many more skills to work with. Time-outs/Take a Break can continue to be effective for children at this age. A good rule of thumb for determining the time a child should "take a break" is one minute for every year old they are, or you can simply end the time when they have calmed down. Doing this, particularly if your child knows it isn't a punishment, will teach self-control as they will understand how taking a break can help them calm down rather than lose control. Creating a "calm-down area" in your home

can help facilitate this process. Include a small table and chair for your child to go to. Add crayons and paper for drawing, make a sensory water bottle filled with a teaspoon of sparkling glitter, water, and a tablespoon of baby oil or cooking oil that they can shake up and then watch the sprinkles fall to the bottom; include items like play dough and stress balls for squeezing and a small stuffed animal for snuggling. You can stay near your child and tell them you are there for them and you will talk to them when they are calm. It's also important to remember to praise your child when they do not lose control in difficult or frustrating situations by saying things like, "I like how you stayed calm" or "Great job keeping your cool."

Distractions can also be helpful for this age group too. If your child becomes upset and is having a difficult time settling down, try distracting them by talking to them about something they enjoy. For example, "Do you remember when we went to Disney World? That was so fun! What did you like the most?" This can help them shift their focus and begin to calm down.

- **School-aged children** can better understand the consequences of their actions and appreciate when they have made good or poor choices. The older the child, the more you can engage in conversation, discussing the consequences of their actions and what they could do differently the next time they feel out of control. Another strategy is to teach your child to imagine a stop sign when they feel they are losing control. This type of visual stimuli can help train them to recognize when certain behaviors require a pause. You could also work on teaching your children to think before they react. Teach them to take a pause or create a space for themselves. A great way to do this is by counting slowly to ten and then taking two quick breaths in through your nose. Another helpful strategy is teaching your child to walk away from stressful situations. Consider the self-control example where you're facing the desire to hit someone and having to deal with anger towards them. As adults, we know walking away and cooling off is a great strategy. Try to avoid showing your frustrations in front of your children, too. Instead, tell your child you are frustrated and need a break to calm down. Modeling this skill for your child can be very powerful.

While these are some of the main strategies for self-control by age, let's look at other critical strategies for developing self-control.

STRATEGIES FOR TEACHING SELF-CONTROL

1. Create Opportunities for Children to Take the Initiative

Giving children some sense of control over their lives is empowering—as it is empowering for adults to feel that they have some control over what is happening. As much as possible, consider what you can do to create opportunities for your child to make decisions about their lives.

2. Keep Their Environment as Stress-Free as Possible

This is not always possible but try to reduce the stress in your child's life whenever you can. This will help minimize their issues with self-control in the long run. A good strategy to accomplish this is to reduce the number of outside-of-school activities your child participates in. These days, there are so many programs available for young kids that it can be tempting to sign them up for multiple activities. Remember that school is a long day for most kids, and being able to go home to relax and unwind at the end of a long school day will be valuable for your child. Having some unstructured free time is so important for kids!

3. Don't Worry If It Doesn't Always Go to Plan

As much as it is helpful to try to minimize stress around your child, you can also teach them to accept mistakes and that things don't always go to plan by showing them how you respond to situations that don't work out how you thought they would. This is an excellent opportunity to teach problem-solving skills. For example, let your child hear you think aloud when things go wrong. For instance, you could say, "Oh no, Starbucks is out of my favorite drink! What am I going to do? I know! I can try a different drink today, and maybe they will have my favorite drink tomorrow." Although this example is a minor disappointment, by thinking out loud, you are showing your child how you came up with a plan B and easily handled the situation.

4. What Would Your Future Self Say?

Another strategy for teaching self-control is to help your child understand that the relative importance of situations can shift. This is true in many instances, but we are often too ready to think that a given situation is critical when in reality, the issue will not be anywhere near as stressful later on. I often used this strategy in college when I didn't get the grade I hoped for on an exam. When I started feeling overwhelmed about my grade, I would ask myself, "Will it really matter five years from now what grade I got on this test?" And the answer was almost always no! This strategy helps put things into perspective and reminds us to focus on the bigger picture, not just the little moments.

5. Use Chores to Encourage a Sense of Responsibility

Giving your children chores isn't about punishment—or it shouldn't be. You can use chores to teach your child to achieve self-control. For example, if your child gets upset about what you are making for dinner, consider giving them the option to help with menu planning or to help make dinner. It will provide them with a sense of control. Here are a few ideas for age-appropriate chores for children:

Ages 2–3	Ages:4–5	Ages:6–7
• Put toys into a toy box • Stack books on a shelf • Place dirty clothes in a hamper • Throw trash away • Fold washcloths • Set the table • Get diapers and wipes • Dust baseboards	• Feed pets • Wipe up spills • Put away toys • Make the bed • Water houseplants • Sort clean silverware • Prepare simple snacks • Use a handheld vacuum • Clear kitchen table • Dry and put away dishes	• Gather trash • Fold towels • Dust mop floors • Empty dishwasher • Match clean socks • Weed garden • Rake leaves • Peel potatoes or carrots • Make a salad • Replace toilet paper roll

Ages 8–9	Ages 10–11	Ages 12 and Up
• Load dishwasher • Wash laundry • Hang/fold clean clothes • Dust furniture • Put groceries away • Scramble eggs • Wipe off tables • Walk the dog • Sweep porch	• Clean bathrooms • Vacuum rugs • Clean countertops • Prepare simple meals • Mow lawn • Bring in mail • Sweep out garage	• Mop floors • Wash/vacuum car • Cook complete dinner • Wash windows • Iron clothes • Watch younger siblings

6. Set Boundaries

Boundaries are not about punishment, either. Kids benefit from having a sense of containment and a sense of limits. Setting boundaries for your kids about what they can and cannot do helps to give them a sense of safety, and that sense of safety, in turn, will help them with self-control. Dr. Siggie Cohen gives excellent advice when she reminds us that boundaries are not questions. For example, when your child makes a poor choice and hits a sibling when they are upset, we often will ask them, "Why did you do that?" This is tricky for young kids because they genuinely cannot tell you why they did something. Instead, try to state boundaries simply, clearly, and directly. So, this might sound like, "No hitting your sister. Even when you are upset. It's okay to feel angry at her. Use a different way to let her know that's not hitting" (Cohen, 2024). Boundaries are also non-negotiable. Make sure your child understands that you are in charge of setting the parameters and that it's not up for discussion because you are the trusted, reliable leader in their life, and you know what is best for them.

7. Support Young Children with Timely Reminders

As much as the goal is to help our children learn to manage their schedules and take care of their responsibilities, we can guide them in this process by using reminders. Reminders and count-downs help to manage expectations about tasks and transitions from one activity to another. They help with routines. Routines are essential for children as they provide security and calmness.

8. Nurture Their Self-Awareness

Encourage your children to develop self-awareness by helping them and rewarding them for articulating how they feel in each moment and identifying strategies to help them calm down and self-regulate. We will talk about this again when we discuss strategies for self-regulation in the next chapter, but it is an important step for self-control.

9. Encourage Regular Mindfulness Practice

To help nurture self-awareness, encourage your children to practice mindfulness. Again, we will revisit this with self-regulation, but mindfulness practices, including meditation and journaling, can help older children develop self-control skills.

10. Be an "Emotion Coach"

In addition to practicing mindfulness, you can model emotional awareness and teach it to your child by serving as an emotion coach. This could involve helping them articulate and label their feelings. I highly recommend the book *A Little Spot of Feelings* by Diane Alber to help kids learn about and label their emotions. We often think children automatically know what different emotions are, but these are words we actively need to teach our kids.

11. Play Games That Help Develop Self-control

Simon Says, Duck, Duck, Goose, and Statutes—are some fun games you can play with your kids to encourage self-control, particularly since they require physical control. Here are a few more fun suggestions:

Freeze-Dance Games

Utilize YouTube to find freeze-dance videos for kids. Some of my favorite freeze-dance videos are the "Party Freeze-Dance Song" by Kiboomers and Danny Go, "Fire and Ice Freeze-Dance."

Don't Eat the Marshmallow

I first saw this activity on a TV show! This experiment was initially developed in the late 1960s to study delayed gratification in children. It is a fun activity to try with your child, and you can do it with kids as young as three years old. Here's how it works:

- In a room with little to no distractions (no TV, toys, or devices), sit your child at a table and give them a plate with a single marshmallow.
- Tell your child you will be leaving the room to complete a quick task and you will return in a moment. While they wait for you, they have two choices: they can eat the marshmallow now or wait to eat it when you come back into the room. If they wait until you return, you will give them two marshmallows to eat.
- Once you leave the room, your child can contemplate the choices you gave them. This will give them time to consider the pros and cons of acting on their initial desire. After all, good things come to those who wait! You can watch a cute video of this experiment on YouTube by searching "The Marshmallow Experiment—instant gratification."

Red Light, Green Light

This is a classic gym class/recess game. To play this game, call out "green light," and your child can take a step forward, but if you call out "red light," they need to freeze.

Once your child is familiar with this game, you can turn it into a helpful impulse control activity. You can tell your child to picture a traffic light in their mind and check the light before they act on an impulse. This traffic light is their light and their light only. Explain that they can make better decisions by paying attention to their imaginary traffic light. Role-play situations and ask them what their traffic light is telling them. If the light turns red, this means their brain is telling them to stop. And for a good reason: to avoid getting hurt or getting into trouble. If the light is yellow, it means to slow down and think carefully about their next choice. I suggest they get help from a parent or teacher at this point. If the light is green, they have determined that their decision is good, and they can proceed while feeling good about their choice.

The No Talking Game

This game works great in a classroom or with siblings. To play this game, start when your family is in an upbeat mood. The goal of this game is to go as long as possible without talking or moving out of your seat. Encourage your kids to listen to their environment and give them a pencil and paper to record all the sounds they hear during the game. The first person to talk ends the game. Challenge your kids to extend the amount of time they can go without talking the next time they play.

12. Encourage Children to Practice Planning

Planning—another of the seven skills we will cover in this book— is also a critical strategy for self-control. Everything from checklists to timetables and schedules will help your children learn to manifest self-control because they can appreciate what will happen and when. Just as having your child help with menu planning can help manage resistance to certain foods, having them learn to plan activities for themselves can help, too.

13. Use Storybooks to Teach Self-control

Here are some of my favorite books for teaching self-control:

- *My Mouth is a Volcano* by Julia Cook
- *I Have Ants in My Pants* by Julia Cook
- *My Magical Choices* by Becky Cummings
- *Even Superheroes Have Bad Days* by Shelly Becker
- *It's Hard to Be Five* by Jamie Lee Curtis and Laura Cornell
- *Breathe Like a Bear* by Kira Willey
- *A Little Spot of Patience* by Diane Alber
- *Clark the Shark* by Bruce Hale and Guy Francis
- *When Sophie Gets Angry—Really, Really Angry* by Molly Bang
- *You Get What You Get* by Julie Gassman
- *The Way I Act* by Steve Metzger

BE AWARE OF THE LINKS BETWEEN SCREEN TIME AND POOR SELF-CONTROL SKILLS

When scientists follow little kids as they grow up, they keep seeing the same worrying pattern: Kids who spend a lot of time using screens tend to do worse on tests that measure their ability to control themselves. For instance, in one study, two-year-olds who spent more time watching TV and playing with touch screens had lower scores on tests that required them to focus, pay attention, and control themselves when they were tested a year later.

I would like to share a simple screen time checklist I discovered from Dr. Jazmine at the Mom Psychologist that I really love. It breaks the day down into morning and late afternoon and also gives some suggestions for holiday screen time. She emphasizes that the items on the checklist are not "rules." It is a tool to use to construct an intentional routine that works for you and your child (McCoy, 2020). Let's take a look!

Mornings:

- Dressed for the day
- Teeth brushed
- Bed is made
- Pajamas are put away
- Backpack is packed (even try doing this the night before)
- Eat breakfast
- Dressed and shoes on
- 10–20 minutes of reading and/or play

If yes to all of these items? It's time for screens.

After school:

- Unpacked backpack
- 30+ minutes of outside play
- Finished homework
- 20+ minutes of reading and/or play
- Family contributions (a.k.a. chores) done
- Showers done and pajamas on

All yes? It's time for screens.

Weekends/Holidays

- Dressed for the day
- Teeth brushed
- Bed is made
- Pajamas are put away
- 20 minutes of reading

- 30 minutes of creative play
- 30 minutes of quiet/alone time
- 30 minutes of outdoor play
- Completed family contributions

All yes? It's time for screens.

Determining how much screen time can be tricky! The American Academy of Pediatrics suggests the following guidelines:

- **Under 2 years old:** Zero screen time, except for video chatting with family or friends
- **2–5 years old:** No more than one hour per day co-viewing with a parent or sibling
- **5–17 years old:** Generally, no more than two hours per day, except for homework

In addition, the American Academy of Pediatrics suggests having a bedroom without screens. This means not having any TVs, phones, or tablets in there. It's also a good idea for kids not to look at screens for at least two hours before going to bed. This is because the blue light from screens can confuse the brain and make it hard to fall asleep. Instead of watching TV, it's better for kids to do something else, like reading a book. Parents and caregivers can also visit the website, www.healthychildren.org, to help them create a media use plan that is right for their family (American Academy of Pediatrics, 2021).

CONCLUSION

Self-control is a cornerstone in the intricate structure of executive functioning, influencing a child's daily interactions, emotions, and overall well-being. The journey through this chapter has underscored the vital role self-control plays in various aspects of a child's life, as exemplified through Ben's struggles and experiences.

By understanding the components of self-control, recognizing signs of its absence, and appreciating the contributing factors, parents and caregivers gain valuable insights into the complexities their children may face. Beyond specific techniques, the broader concepts of fostering agency, setting boundaries, and embracing mistakes as opportunities for growth are fundamental to developing strong self-control skills. A child's brain is like a sponge, and they will use their ever-changing environment to make decisions. Strong impulse control will boost the likelihood that they will make better decisions as they develop as teenagers and grow through adulthood. Another critical factor to consider is impulsivity. When we teach our kids to become aware of their actions and how they affect those around them, they will also begin to notice that, like them, other kids may also lack self-control. This awareness helps develop empathy. This is a powerful tool for teaching our kids valuable life skills, such as pausing to think before acting. As parents and caregivers begin nurturing self-control in their children, they not only contribute to the enhancement of executive functioning but also lay the groundwork for empowered decision-making and a resilient sense of self.

In the next chapter, we will dive into super skill number two, self-regulation, and begin to realize that each skill serves as a thread woven into the fabric of a child's cognitive and emotional development.

SUPER SKILL #2: SELF-REGULATION

"When little people are overwhelmed by big emotions, it's our job to share our calm, not join their chaos."

— *L.R. KNOST*

L et's return to the story of Ben.

BEN'S STORY

As a sixth grader, Ben has a lot on his plate. He must juggle the demands of home and school. He knows that his parents expect a lot from him, and he wants to live up to those expectations in his interactions with teachers and peers at school. He's also acutely aware of how he can lose focus, even control when frustrated. He struggles to manage his impulses, and when he loses control, he tends to spiral. Things get bad quickly. Very quickly. When he's deregulated and can't focus, he starts to play around in class. If he plays around in class, he gets in trouble with his teacher, which increases his anxiety. He tends to crave stimulation, and that leads him to act out. At the same time, though, his behaviors are getting him into trouble, and he is being punished for the outbursts or banned from going outside during regular class breaks. These are all issues related to the problem of self-regulation, which is, like self-control, something that many people, particularly adults, take for granted.

SELF-REGULATION AT A GLANCE

But what exactly is self-regulation? It is a skill that allows people to control their emotions, behavior, and body movements in the face of difficult situations. It also allows them to do this while remaining focused and alert. Many children, and even a fair number of adults, struggle with self-regulation. In emotional situations, people can act impulsively. In hindsight, they can say what they should have done differently. However, the problem remains that they couldn't prevent themselves from doing the wrong thing, which they felt overwhelmingly compelled to do when they were in the moment. Of course, it's easy to confuse self-regulation with self-control. They are undoubtedly related concepts, but it is important to distinguish between them.

As we discussed, self-control is primarily a social skill. As outlined in the previous chapter, it's the big lesson kids learn early in school. They don't just go to school to learn their ABCs but also to learn how to sit quietly during lessons, share with others, follow directions, and to get started on their schoolwork in a timely manner.

Self-regulation, by contrast, has to do with the physical regulation of the body. One of the best analogies is to think of the body as a room with a thermostat. The goal of the thermostat is to keep the room at the set temperature. If I set the thermostat of my classroom to sixty-five, the heating and cooling systems surrounding the room will kick in when the thermostat indicates that there's a need for warm or cool air in the space. On a hot day when the regular temperature outside keeps climbing, the thermostat must work harder to keep the temperature in the room at the set point. Ditto when it's cold and the temperature outside drops. And even on a mild day, there's fluctuation. The thermostat is constantly checking and regulating to maintain the set temperature. Imagine, then, that the thermostat isn't working. That's a child with self-regulation issues. The thermostat doesn't sense when the temperature starts to spike, for example, or it does, but it doesn't register the change until the temperature has risen by, say, ten degrees. Suddenly, people are sitting in a room that's too hot, and the thermostat needs to kick in and work double-time to bring the temperature down. Just like our room, we all have a set state or ideal temperature. That's when we're calm and collected. When we're focused and able to engage. We're not feeling too tired or too restless. We have just the right amount of energy to do what we need to do. That's being regulated. As we get older, we also learn to adjust when certain conditions change—when we feel that we can't focus, are too tired, or can't sit still for too long.

Imagine a time when you had to focus on something but realized you were too tired to do it. What did you do? Chances are good that you got up and walked around for a bit. Or you grabbed something to drink—some coffee? —or something to eat. Perhaps you stretched or took a bathroom break. Whatever it was, I'll bet that strategy helped you to get back to what you needed to do. You self-regulated. And while we adults are generally able to self-regulate, it's a skill kids have to learn. There are also those who have regulation disorders, finding it hard to figure out exactly what they need at any given time to calm down or to stay focused on a task. For kids and those with regulatory issues, the process of self-regulation can be a tricky one to learn, and it's not something many schools focus on. Parents rarely know how to teach this skill, either!

Long story short, self-regulation is a critical component of children's development that enables them to control their emotions, behavior, and energy levels based on situational demands. In practice, it is particularly important to academic success in the long term because it involves resisting highly emotional reactions to upsetting stimuli, calming down when upset, being flexible to change, and handling frustration without outbursts.

As with those who learn self-control, children who learn self-regulation are better equipped to cope with anxiety and frustration, are more likely to succeed academically and achieve long-term goals, and are less resistant to environmental changes, making them more resilient. Children with well-developed self-regulation skills can also handle stress better and cope with challenges, enabling them to focus, learn, and develop healthy relationships. In reality, kids who can self-regulate have the skills to remove themselves from challenging situations and the ability to readjust when they know they can't focus. Considering the school setting and our example of Ben, self-regulation is especially crucial for children who struggle with impulse control or managing their big emotions. After all, sensory processing involves noting sensations, as well as, blocking out anything that is not needed. Once a person can do this, they can focus during activities. Self-regulation is also deeply connected to a child's attention, how aware they are, and how they react. The obvious problem for kids who have sensory processing issues, and for young kids in general, is that they often have no idea how to do this. Young kids especially don't know they should be calm and focused because it's time for math class or story time at the library. If they are starting school for the first time, they have no idea how this sort of routine works. Kids also don't tend to care that they're full of energy at 9 p.m. when they should be getting ready for bed because they have to wake up at 6 a.m. If they're overstimulated, they'll keep going, bouncing around or talking, crying, or running around. Multiply this by ten for people with sensory processing issues who have trouble handling information that comes in through one or more of their senses.

Stimuli affecting self-regulation include anything involving sight, smell, hearing, taste, and touch. Still, there is also interoception (sensing signals from the body like being hungry or needing to go to the bathroom), proprioception (the body's ability to perceive movement, action, and location, like knowing your feet are on soft grass and not cement without looking), and the vestibular sense (the body's ability to maintain balance during movements) to consider, as these also affect the body's nervous system. If we think back to the case of Ben, part of what will be problematic for him is all the sensory input he has to manage when he is in the classroom. For many kids with sensory processing issues and those lacking self-regulation skills, being in a classroom space, which is often noisy and full of visual stimuli, can be overwhelming.

Consider, for a minute, your average classroom. There are usually about twenty-five kids. The younger the kids, the more likely there will be a fair amount of noise. You've also got sounds from furniture moving, teachers talking, and appliances in the classroom. Then there's the visual stimuli. Many teachers put posters on the walls—vocabulary words, basic math concepts, maps. While these are important learning tools and help create a positive vibe for the classroom overall, the visual stimuli are a lot for kids who struggle to regulate. There's also a lot of sensory information—the surfaces of tables, the floor, the chairs, and different smells. All this stuff can again add to the information a child has to process. When the system is already overwhelmed, it is like messing with the thermostat and letting the temperature climb.

HOW TO SPOT A CHILD WHO IS STRUGGLING WITH SELF-REGULATION

1. Has a Difficult Time with Transitions

This could look like having a hard time leaving an exciting environment like a playdate or birthday party, trouble getting out the door in the morning on time or getting stuck on activities such as watching TV or playing on an iPad.

2. Plays Too Rough

Some examples include when roughhousing with friends or siblings turns into biting, when pushing turns into shoving, or when touching turns into tackling. In these situations, the child is unaware that things have gone too far, and that they need to calm down or stop.

3. Has Frequent Meltdowns

A child might react strongly to little problems or when things don't go as planned. They might seem like they're losing control or moving their body around a lot. This happens when they're overwhelmed with what they see, hear, or feel. It's like their brain gets too full, and they can't handle more. Their reactions might be bigger than you would expect.

4 Has Difficulty Socializing with Peers

It can be hard for the child to play with others or share toys. Making friends can be tricky for them. They might need help understanding their friends' actions or miss social cues. You might find yourself having to step in a lot when they play with kids their age.

5. Struggles with Daily Routines

This could look like getting wound up right before bedtime and finding it hard to fall asleep. They might have a tough time waking up in the morning or often wake up feeling grumpy. Sometimes, they might struggle to stay seated during meals, making it hard to finish eating.

Regarding timing, self-regulation needs to be something we start to see as a foundational skill in early child development, beginning in infancy and continuing into adulthood. Developing self-regulation skills can benefit children in the future by giving them a solid foundation for successfully setting, managing, and achieving their goals in life. It is honestly a skill that they need to be working on from a very young age. It's one of those skills that parents and teachers must start prioritizing along with literacy and math skills in early childhood. Caregivers can support the development of self-regulation by helping kids recognize goals, removing unnecessary demands, guiding them with loving support, and providing strategies and opportunities to practice remaining calm and collected in stressful situations. In other words, self-regulation is a skill that needs to be taught explicitly and practiced by children.

So, now that we have an idea of what self-regulation is and why we need it, let's talk about how to teach it. What strategies can we use to help children learn to self-regulate, particularly when they may have issues with self-regulation and are too young to sense their needs automatically? Once kids can articulate how they are feeling, that's when you can start introducing different strategies to encourage self-regulation. As you can probably appreciate, effective strategies for parents and educators to enhance self-regulation skills in children are crucial for children's success and happiness in life and are integral to academic success. A well-regulated kid is a focused kid, end of story. Here are some great strategies to try with children:

STRATEGIES AND TIPS FOR TEACHING SELF-REGULATION

1. Teach Self-Awareness

Encourage kids to articulate what they are feeling at any given point, particularly when they are beginning to feel overwhelmed by sensory stimuli. The most common symptoms of deregulation are being overly excited or stimulated, excessively tired, hungry, thirsty, or bored. Both parents and teachers can help children learn to articulate their feelings by first keeping track of behavior patterns. This part starts with parents, as they will have spent the most time with their kids in the beginning. Remember how, when your child was a baby, you learned to figure out when they were hungry or tired? This same idea holds true for teaching self-regulation by first helping your child be attuned to their feelings.

2. Pay Attention to Patterns

There will be times when your child is tired, hungry, or thirsty, for example, and they will tend to get ill-tempered or restless. If you can track those times and encourage your child to articulate how they feel, you can start the recognition process so that they can notice the symptoms and self-advocate when you aren't around.

3. Teach Breathing and Meditation Skills

Parents and educators can help children learn and practice self-regulation skills by providing them with opportunities to practice calming techniques like deep breathing and mindfulness activities. It is also helpful to encourage them to use positive self-talk to regulate their emotions. I love the book *My Magic Breath* by Nick Ortner for helping kids understand the power of breathing and how to use it to calm the mind. This book is an excellent tool for parents and teachers because the story actively involves children while teaching them valuable techniques. Here are a few of my favorite breathing exercises to try:

Starfish Breathing

Stretch your hand wide like a starfish. With your other hand, use your finger to draw around your fingers, starting at your wrist. Breathe in through your nose as you move up from the side of your thumb and breathe out of your mouth as you move down. Keep doing this around your hand until you have traced the entire "starfish." If your child is sensitive to touch or finds it hard to starfish breathe for some other reason, try belly breathing instead.

Belly Breathing

Lie on your back on the floor and place your hand on your tummy. Take a big breath in through your nose, counting "one hippopotamus, two hippopotamus, three hippopotamus," and feel your hand go up. Then, breathe out through your mouth for three seconds and feel your hand go down. Do this four times in a row.

Pretzel Breaths

The "pretzel" involves taking deep breaths AND a specific body posture. The posture can either be crossing your arms (hugging yourself) or extending your arms outward, crossing them with palms together, interlacing your fingers, and inverting your hands toward your body. Once in the pose, take several deep breaths until you feel calm. This is a fantastic calming technique because it requires you to cross the right and left sides of the body. According to Dr. Becky Bailey's Conscious Discipline program, when the right and left sides are crossed, BOTH sides of your brain are actively engaged and more focused on what you are trying to achieve (Conscious Discipline 2020).

4. Teach Yoga

Yoga for kids can be a great way to teach children how to calm their bodies down after a busy day or activity. I love "Cosmic Kids Yoga" and "Salamander Yoga" by Scratch Garden; both are free on YouTube. I use these videos with my kindergarten class when I notice my students are tired or need a break from academics. It helps to explain why we practice these things with our kids. I point out to my students that Yoga is a healthy way to help our bodies relax and feel calm.

5. Model Self-Regulation Skills

Think out loud around our kids. For example, if you are feeling stressed out about household chores, you could say, "I'm feeling like I need to take a break from my chores for a minute. Let's take a walk outside and get some fresh air. Then I will feel better and have more energy to finish my work."

6. Create Predictable Routines

Predictability helps children feel secure and, in turn, will help to regulate their emotions. Here are a few ideas of important routines to develop with your kids:

- Getting ready in the morning
- Eating meals
- Spending time playing and talking together
- Reading books or telling stories
- Bath time and getting ready for bed

7. Use Visual Aids

Visual aids, such as a "zones of regulation chart," can be used to help children understand and regulate their emotions. This chart shows four colored sections: blue for the feelings of sick, tired, sad, and bored; green for happy, calm, and focused; yellow for frustrated, worried, silly, and excited; and red for mad, angry, and out of control. Each colored space on the poster can also have a character showing the emotion. Have you ever seen the Disney movie *Inside Out?* This movie has the perfect characters to go along with a zones of regulation chart! Parents and teachers can display a zones of regulation chart in an area where they can easily reference it throughout the day. Parents can coach children through tough situations using the chart to help them identify their feelings instead of avoiding them. Be sure to praise their efforts when they try practicing self-regulation skills and when they attempt to label their emotions. Zones of regulation charts can be found on websites like Temu, Etsy, and Amazon.

8. Remember to Practice Skills When Your Child is Calm

If your child is melting down or experiencing really big emotions, wait until they have calmed down. Then, you can go back and talk about what happened and go over some strategies for when they have those feelings.

9. Teach Consequences and Always Follow Through

Because difficulties with poor self-regulation skills can result in challenging behaviors, it's important for children to recognize that poor behavior has consequences and to know what those consequences will be. Cultivating a warm and loving relationship with children is an effective strategy for parents and educators to help their children develop healthy self-regulation skills, as kids who feel secure enough to practice new skills and learn from their mistakes cope more effectively in times of stress. By building positive relationships with children, providing extra support, and scaffolding their learning, parents and educators can enhance self-regulation skills in children, which will help them cope with and adapt to change, achieve their goals, and avoid negative consequences.

10. Try the 5-4-3-2-1 Method

This handy technique helps young kids become more aware of their surroundings and how they feel. By practicing 5-4-3-2-1, you can shift their focus away from worries and onto what's happening around them. Here's how it works:

Spot and identify:

- **5** things they can see, like their favorite toy, a colorful picture, or a fluffy pillow
- **4** things they can touch or feel, such as the softness of a stuffed animal, the smoothness of a book cover, or the warmth of a blanket
- **3** things they can hear, like birds chirping outside, the hum of a fan, or the sound of their own breathing

- **2** things they can smell, maybe a whiff of cookies baking or the scent of flowers
- **1** thing they can taste, even if it's just a tiny bite of their snack

11. Teach Positive Affirmations

Affirmations are like magical words that can make kids feel strong and happy, even when things are tough. Help them come up with affirmations they can say to themselves. For older kids, writing their affirmation on a sticky note and posting it in a place they can see it throughout the day will help them remember their positive thoughts.

Here are a few examples of good affirmations for kids to try:

- "I am brave."
- "I know I can do this."
- "I can do hard things."
- "I choose to be happy and have fun."
- "I can learn anything I want to learn."
- "I am smart and capable."
- "I know it's okay to make mistakes."

12. Go for a Stroll

Taking a walk can be a fun adventure for kids and help them feel better when they're upset. Whether it's a walk in the park or around the house, the fresh air and movement can help them feel calm. You can even turn it into a game by spotting birds or counting flowers.

13. Rock or Sway

Sometimes, when feelings get too big, rocking or swaying can make kids feel calm again. Kids can try rocking in a cozy chair, swaying gently to their favorite song, or rolling on the floor like a playful animal.

14. Express Feelings through Art or Words

Drawing pictures or talking about how they feel can be an excellent way for kids to understand and manage their emotions. Encourage them to draw what makes them happy, sad, or excited or to tell you about their day in their own words. Journaling, drawing, or even talking out loud to themselves are all things that can help your child self-monitor. To get started, use "draw what you see in your mind" as a prompt. Seeing or hearing what's in your head can help children step back from what they are worried about. It can separate facts from feelings and allow them to think about how to deal with a problem. Often, it's less about figuring out a solution and more about understanding what seems so overwhelming. These simple techniques are designed to help young kids navigate their feelings and find calmness in the midst of big emotions.

15. Teach Kids about the "Mind Table"

I first learned about the mind table from reading an article on child therapist, Jess Vanderwier's blog, Nurtured First. Jess explains that when your child has a big worry, such as spiders crawling into their bed at night, have them imagine a big table with a lot of chairs. At one seat, there is someone named Worry. In the other chairs are Anger, Excitement, Jealousy, and Sadness. And at the end of the table, there is someone strong and tall—it's them!

They are the boss of their own mind table! Explain that sometimes, Worry can help you and keep you safe. But sometimes, Worry takes over. Worry isn't the boss of your mind. You are! In our spider example above, you could encourage your child to state their worry out loud and then put worry in its place by saying, "Worry, sit down! I don't need to think about spiders right now! I'm safe!" Next, have your child draw a picture of their mind table. Have them draw themselves sitting at the head of the table, telling Worry to sit down. Draw the other emotions sitting at the table, too. Hang their picture up so they can see it and be reminded that they are the boss of their mind (Vanderwier 2024). This visualization can give kids the power they need to feel in control of their emotions.

My favorite executive function guru, Tera Sumpter, lays out a few more key tips to consider when teaching kids self-regulation skills (Sumpter 2023d):

Telling Kids What to Do All the Time Will Slow Down the Development of Self-Regulation

For example, telling your child to pay attention is not helping them notice anything about their behavior or environment. If you think about it, if you always had someone telling you what to do, you will always need to rely on that input to accomplish anything. Instead, we need to teach kids to build self-awareness by helping them notice their thoughts, which leads to Tera's next point.

Use Reflexive Questioning

Using questions like:

- What are we doing right now?
- Is what you are doing right now part of this activity?
- What do you think will happen if you do that?

These types of questions will help build your child's awareness of the situation, and with continued practice, they will learn how to ask themselves these important questions.

An added benefit of reflexive questions is that there are no wrong answers. You can praise kids for their answers or ask another question. Let's use this conversation as an example:

Adult: What activity are you doing right now?

Child: Brushing my teeth!

Adult: That's right! I'm glad you know that! Is playing with your car part of brushing your teeth?

Child: No.

Adult: Right! What should you be doing right now?

Child: Putting toothpaste on my brush.

Adult: Awesome! Can you show me?

This type of interaction is much more productive than repeatedly telling your child to brush their teeth, and it builds trust that they can be in charge of themselves and make the right choices.

The big takeaway is that developing self-regulation skills in children at an early age requires a supportive framework and coaching from parents and other caregivers. It requires consistency and compassion. Strategies for developing self-regulation skills also vary considerably by age. Therefore, it's essential to consider the child's age and developmental level and choose appropriate methods. For example, child development researchers have documented there can be biological and genetic reasons behind the variation in self-regulation skills, and they will note that very young children actually lack some of the basic skills to recognize when they are feeling dysregulated. It is also vital to match behavior expectations to the child's age and stage of development to avoid the frustration that comes along with not having the skills or understanding to do what they're asked. Younger children have less developed brains and are less able to regulate themselves. Between twelve and eighteen months, children become aware of social demands and have the ability to change their behavior when a parent asks. Still, before this, they will be unable to register a social situation that requires them to behave a certain way—not even in the most basic sense. At three years old, for example, children begin to generalize self-regulation strategies from previous experiences and act in a way that reflects how they think their parents would want them to act in different situations. Therefore, caregivers of children about this age must assess their skills to determine where they need support. These findings only apply to children exhibiting typical development tracks. For kids who struggle with executive function and self-regulation skills and who will likely be behind their peers on these developmental milestones, extra support is necessary to help them catch up.

It's also essential to remember that kids don't develop self-regulation skills overnight; it's a lifelong process. Some adults *without* sensory processing issues, who have self-regulation skills, will give way to feeling dysregulated sometimes. Even adults lose their temper or act out, and we need to remember this when we're dealing with kids and expecting them to develop and apply these skills. Even as experienced users, we sometimes fail to use them, too.

GAMES THAT HELP BUILD SELF-REGULATION SKILLS

1. Exploding Emotions: Ages 6+
2. Who's Feeling What? By Learning Resources: Ages 3+
3. My Feelings Game-Exploring Emotions Through Fun, Active Play: Ages 4+

STORYBOOKS TO READ TO CHILDREN ABOUT SELF-REGULATION

1. *Llama Llama Mad at Mama* by Anna Dewdney
2. *When Sophie Gets Angry—Really, Really Angry* by Molly Bang
3. *Bear Feels Scared* by Karma Wilson
4. *Bye Bye Pesky Fly* by Lysa Mullady
5. *Grumpy Bird* by Jeremy Tankard
6. *Wemberly Worried* by Kevin Henkes
7. *I am Thankful* by Sheri Wall
8. *I Feel Happy: Why Do I Feel Happy Today?* by DK
9. *Marvelous Me: Inside and Out* by Lisa Bullard
10. *Bored Claude* by Jill Newton
11. *I'm Sad* by Michael Ian Black
12. *When Sophie's Feelings Are Really, Really Hurt* by Molly Bang
13. *Glad Monster, Sad Monster* by Ed Emberley
14. *The Color Monster* by Anna Llenas
15. *The Feelings Book* by Todd Parr
16. *A Little Spot of Patience* by Diane Alber
17. *Breathe Like a Bear* by Kira Willey
18. *Even Superheroes Have Bad Days* by Shelly Becker
19. *You Get What You Get* by Julia Gassman
20. *The Pigeon Has Feelings Too!* by Mo Willems

CONCLUSION

As we have discussed in this chapter, self-regulation, like self-control, is crucial for success in various aspects of life, including academics, personal relationships, and overall well-being. Self-regulation involves the ability to manage your thoughts, emotions, and behaviors in a way that promotes positive outcomes. Self-regulation is connected to how our brains grow, especially the part called the prefrontal cortex. This part keeps growing even into adulthood. It's important to remember that self-regulation is tough for young kids and even harder when they are tired or stressed out. Adults need to keep this information in mind so we can have appropriate expectations for our kids and what they are capable of doing. Kids learn how to regulate their emotions through a process called "co-regulation." Co-regulation means when someone supports us by helping us understand our emotions and how to control them. Your child learns to manage their feelings by getting help from others and watching you handle your own emotions calmly. This can be hard sometimes, but it's important to remember that taking care of yourself is necessary for you to support your child's development in the best way possible. In this chapter, we've explored the definition and importance of self-regulation strategies, the benefits of implementing them, and the challenges individuals may face when applying them consistently.

The next chapter will explore super skill number three, adaptable thinking. We will discuss the importance of adaptable thinking as a strategy to help your child negotiate their way through the day and manage instances where they must change their plans or ideas under pressure.

SUPER SKILL #3: ADAPTABLE THINKING

"The measure of intelligence is the ability to change."

— *ALBERT EINSTEIN*

So, let's return to Ben's story and think about our next skill: adaptable thinking.

We know that Ben sometimes struggles to go about his day because he has trouble with self-control and self-regulation. But he's more likely to have a good day when things go according to a routine that he prefers or is at least familiar with. Why is this? Well, one of the challenges, one of the triggers, especially for people with executive function issues, is having to adapt to change. Change is hard, particularly when you are even a little bit reliant upon a routine to help you stay focused and calm.

BEN'S STRUGGLES WITH ADAPTABLE THINKING

Ben is trying to stay focused on his routine in school. It helps him stay organized and remember what he needs at any given time. He starts his morning with a check-in with his teacher. He then goes to assembly and has two classes before a twenty-minute break. Next, he has gym, followed by lunch. After lunch, there are typically three classes, and they alternate according to what day it is. Today, however, things are not going according to plan. Ben's teacher is out sick, so his check-in meeting with her is canceled. The school also has a special schedule, making the initial schedule disruption much more troublesome. There is a long assembly in the morning, so Ben has to skip his morning classes. He also has to miss gym to make up for the first two classes. Not only does Ben prefer gym over math and English class, but he also needs this time in gym class to run around and release his energy. It helps him regulate. So, missing it makes Ben feel angry.

As Ben tries to work his way through his day with an unusual schedule to contend with, he's finding himself increasingly frustrated and resistant to the changes he must follow. He does not like to do things in new ways, and the more he needs to adapt during the school day, the more his other struggles with self-control and self-regulation become pronounced.

If Ben had the opportunity to develop some strategies for developing adaptable thinking, he would likely have an easier time dealing with changes to his routine.

ADAPTABLE THINKING AT A GLANCE

So, what are adaptable thinking skills, and why are they important for children's development? Just as kids struggle with self-control and self-regulation, children can also have difficulty with adaptable thinking if they haven't been explicitly taught how to do it from a young age. A lack of flexible thinking skills can make taking on new tasks and responsibilities challenging. The good news is that cultivating adaptable thinking skills will provide life-long benefits, such as helping to develop a positive mindset, improving self-regulation, and building stronger social skills. This all leads to better mental health outcomes for children. Also known as flexible thinking, adaptable thinking is crucial for a child's cognitive development for several reasons:

1. These skills allow children to stretch their perceptions and thoughts, accept change and move forward, and reduce the impact of life's ups and downs on their general well-being. Remember how, for Ben, changes to his routine caused further disruption to his self-control and self-regulation?
2. Adaptable thinking skills help children to understand different perspectives, comprehend important information, and move beyond basic ways of doing things. Since flexible thinking also plays an important role in how children learn and adapt to new information, flexible thinking skills can be integral to developing meaningful critical thinking skills.
3. Weak adaptable thinking skills can lead to negative self-talk, an increasingly pessimistic outlook on life, and possibly self-destructive behaviors.

HOW TO SPOT IF A CHILD IS HAVING TROUBLE WITH ADAPTABLE THINKING

Kids who struggle with flexible thinking might find things challenging at home and school. They have a hard time seeing things from different viewpoints or figuring out new ways to solve problems.

Here are some things you might notice at home and school:

- They don't like considering other people's ideas.
- They keep arguing the same point again and again.
- They get upset even if small things don't go as planned.
- They make the same mistakes repeatedly.
- They need help to adjust to new schedules.
- Changes in plans make them anxious.
- They struggle with taking on new, more demanding tasks.
- Switching from one activity to another is tough for them.
- They get upset when others don't follow the rules.
- They may have slower processing speeds.

Let's talk about how some kids, like Ben, find it hard to switch gears. When there's a change in plans, they might feel nervous or angry. They struggle with change because they can only see one-way things should be done. These kids also have a tough time thinking flexibly and having a growth mindset. For example, people with a growth mindset believe they can improve at something by putting in time, effort, and energy. They focus on fixing their weaknesses and care more about the journey than the result. They believe that with practice, they can reach their goals. Developing a growth mindset along with flexible thinking can help kids overcome challenges and learn from failures. This is why being able to think flexibly is such a valuable life skill. We often need to look at things from different angles to solve problems or get along with others. For example, let's say your child's friend cancels a playdate because they're sick. Most of us would think, "That's ok, when can we hang out another time?" or "What else can I do today?" But it's not so simple for kids who struggle with flexible thinking. They might get stuck thinking about the canceled playdate or get really upset because they can't understand why it had to be canceled. Teaching flexible thinking to our kids can help them handle these situations better and be more successful. Let's explore some ways we can teach them this valuable skill.

STRATEGIES FOR TEACHING ADAPTABLE THINKING

1. Give Kids Examples That Demonstrate Flexible and Rigid Thinking

To begin teaching the idea of flexible thinking, it can be very beneficial to explain what it means to be flexible and rigid. Stories can be a nice way to begin a discussion about these topics with young kids. The counselor at my school uses the book *A Little SPOT of Flexible Thinking: A Story about Adapting* to Change by Diane Alber with our kindergarteners. This book helps kids understand what the words flexible and rigid mean. For example, flexible thinking is compared to a swaying palm tree with roots like spaghetti. These trees can sway and bend in the wind. They are flexible. And rigid thinking is compared to an oak tree with a sturdy trunk and roots that are firmly planted in the ground. This type of tree is not very bendable, and the branches could snap in a strong wind. They are rigid. After kids understand these two definitions, they are ready to practice with some scenarios. The website Teachers Pay Teachers has some excellent resources for flexible thinking activities for different age levels. I like the *Flexible Thinking Scenarios All*

Seasons Bundle by a Fresh Breath on Teaching. This bundle gives examples of flexible and rigid thinking by season and asks kids to decide what type of thinking the person is using in each example. The scenarios are ready to print out as cards so they can be used as a game. Practicing a little every week is the perfect way to help kids build their flexible thinking skills.

2. Teach Problem-Solving Skills

Problem-solving requires cognitive flexibility, which enables individuals to think on their feet when things do not go as planned. Adaptable thinking skills are important for doing homework and studying for tests, particularly when switching between subjects during homework time. This becomes increasingly more important as kids get older and have more work to juggle. To make appropriate switches between tasks and subjects, for example, kids need to be able to change their thinking. On the surface, solving math problems requires a strategy different from doing a writing assignment. However, what happens when a math problem presents as a word problem and requires the breakdown of language elements? What about when you must write about something more scientific, more like a process? This can require skills more like those used in solving math problems. If a student struggles to move back and forth between different subject areas and skills, these problems can be hard. Problem-solving skills can help to resolve these difficulties. By learning to approach things differently, they can start to see how skills or approaches don't have to be so rigidly categorized either. They can begin to see that different skills complement each other. They can also become more accustomed to using different skill sets together.

3. Validate Emotions

Managing disappointment or uncertainty is challenging. And that's okay. It's important to validate kids' feelings before trying to move on, no matter how outsized or confusing they may be. For example, "I see how sad you are that your cousins couldn't come visit this year. I know you miss them. I do, too. It's tough." When kids feel heard and understood, they're less likely to dwell on the negative emotions and can better move on to finding a solution.

4. Get Kids Involved

Giving kids a degree of control can help them feel as though they have some opportunity to manage what challenges or frustrates them. It is important to remember that getting from frustration or sadness to acceptance and action takes time and practice.

Kids may respond slower than you'd like them to. When that happens, be patient and encourage kids to try flexible thinking to help manage distress and build resilience. "I can see you're still really missing your cousins. I wonder if there's anything that might help? Maybe we could write them a letter, and you could decorate it?" When kids are ready, invite them to help you come up with ideas for managing uncertainty and difficult changes. For example: "I'm really excited about your birthday party too, but there's a chance we might not be able to have your party outside. Let's think of some awesome ideas for what to do if that happens." When kids feel like part of the plan, they'll have a greater sense of control and get the chance to practice their flexible thinking skills.

5. Teach Kids About Having a Growth Mindset

Growing up can be tough for kids, and they will inevitably face challenges. What really matters during those hard times is their ability to keep trying, even when things get challenging, and to learn from mistakes. It's important for them to be resilient and perseverant in the face of obstacles. One good way to build a positive mindset is to teach kids about the word "yet." For example, if a child says, "I will never be able to ride my bike without training wheels!" Try telling them, "You can't ride your bike without training wheels *yet*, but you can learn to do it." This is a good way to reflect a growth mindset and teach them how to reframe their thoughts. *The Magical Yet* by Angela DiTerlizzi is a wonderful book that will teach kids who get frustrated by what they can't do to keep trying and overcome challenges.

6. Model Flexibility

Children learn a lot from watching how their parents handle things. Showing them good ways to deal with problems, can help both of you handle tough situations better and feel less stressed. One way to do this is by talking out loud about how you're figuring out a problem. For instance, if a friend cancels plans, you can say, "Oh, that's a bummer. Maybe we can plan something else for next time." When kids see you handling changes or surprises calmly and trying to find solutions, they're more likely to do the same. It's also okay for them to see you deal with situations where there's no quick fix. Relying on strategies to reduce your stress levels in the meantime, whether that's going for a walk, listening to music, taking deep breaths, calling a friend, or whatever works for you, shows kids that an uncertain situation doesn't have to feel like a disaster.

7. Help Kids When They Need It

It's harder for kids to be flexible in their thinking when they're dealing with mental health issues like anxiety or depression. Also, if something really traumatic happened to your family, like losing a loved one, a job, or your home, it can make it even more challenging. If you see your child acting more rigid, upset, anxious, or sad than usual, it could mean they're having a tough time with their mental health. Talk to your child about how they're feeling, and consider reaching out to a doctor, therapist, or someone at their school who can give support.

8. Break Down Tasks into Smaller Chunks to Make Them More Doable

To break down tasks, you can use this basic strategy:

- First, calculate how much time your child has to complete their task. In some instances, it will be a matter of minutes or hours. If it is a larger project, count backward from the due date to figure out how many days you have to work on the assignment. Next, determine how long your child can work on the project at a time. For younger children, keeping work sessions limited to relatively short bursts is particularly important. However, even older kids will need breaks and changes in their activities. Challenge your child to work on something for a certain amount of time for non-preferred tasks like homework or chores. For example, ask your child if they can work on their homework for five minutes. Then, the next day, try to extend the time to ten minutes.

- Once you have worked out how much time you have and your work schedule figured out, write down each task with your child using index cards. You should have one card for each task. As you work on each item, you will also want to check in with your child to see if they have any questions or concerns you need to address. These should be written down on the back of the card as well.
- Next, organize the task cards in order. Support your child by helping them work out the appropriate order. Consider the best, most logical sequence for events.
- Once you have the order for the tasks, determine a deadline for each item and do your best to address any questions or concerns your child has about the work. This is the point at which your child will be setting off to work on the individual tasks, and by answering the questions and addressing concerns, you can help get them into the best possible mindset.
- The final step in the process is to make a plan to review your child's progress, checking in with them about the status of the project. You will also want a strategy for revising the plan if things are not progressing as they should. For example, tweak the deadlines if your child struggles to complete things on time.

9. Talk About Plans for the Next Day Ahead of Time

Discuss what the day will look like with your child, and point out some possible challenges that might happen. For example, you could say, "If I'm running late to pick you up from school, you will go to aftercare until I can get there." Knowing there is a plan in case of the unexpected will help your child feel prepared and models for them how to overcome the inevitable curve balls of life!

10. Create Situations Where Your Child Has to Follow Someone Else's Plan

Invite a friend over and have your child take turns with them, deciding on what will be played. When you play with your child, choose a toy, determine how the play will go, and have your child follow along. This is an excellent exercise in helping your child see another person's perspective and will also teach them to adapt to the play scenario.

11. Point Out the Rules and Exceptions of Language When They Occur

Studies show that students with adaptable thinking skills understand both language rules and exceptions, making them more efficient communicators. For instance, understanding that many words change to past tense by adding -ed, like talked, called, and filled, but also being able recognize there are exceptions for some words like sold, made, and went, that don't follow this rule. Pointing out these little nuances in language can be beneficial for kids.

Using wordplay and jokes is also a great way to boost flexible thinking through language. For example, take time to explain that words can have more than one meaning. I love to teach this by reading the *Amelia Bedelia* books by Peggy and Herman Parish. The main character in these stories takes everything literally. For example, when asked to "draw the curtains," she draws a picture of them. This creates a wonderful opportunity to discuss what she should have done instead and how words can have more than one meaning. Another way to help kids understand the flexible nature of language is to have fun telling jokes that play with the meanings and sounds of words. For example: "Why are fish so smart? Because they live in schools!" Explain how the punchline uses two meanings of the word school. A fun joke book to try is *The Big Book of Silly Jokes for Kids* by Carole Roman. Change can also be reframed using language. For instance, when there is a change to routine, language describing the sequence of events, "first this, then that," can be used to guide acceptance of changes.

12. Change the Rules of Favorite Games

Demonstrate for your child that games can be played in multiple ways and that this can be fun! Start with simple switches in games kids know well, like Chutes and Ladders. Instead of climbing up the ladders and sliding down the chutes, agree to slide down the ladders and go up the chutes!

13. Find More Than One Way to Do Everyday Things

Challenge your child to get dressed in a different order than they usually would or have them help you come up with a different route to drive to school.

14. Make an Achievement Jar

This is a fun way to help kids feel good about what they've learned and encourage them to keep trying new things. Here's how you can make one:

- Get a jar or a box and some small pieces of paper and let your child design a label for the jar.
- Ask your child to think about things they couldn't do before but learned how to do by practicing and not giving up, like riding a bike or learning something new at school.

- Write each of these achievements on a piece of paper and put them in the jar.
- Every week, your child can add new achievements to the jar, even if they're small ones.

Once in a while, take out all the papers from the jar, read them together, and celebrate each achievement. This will help your child feel proud and more confident about learning new things.

15. Praise the Effort and Not the Result

Research has shown that it's more beneficial to praise how hard someone tries rather than just praising what they achieve. Many studies have proven that praising only the results causes more harm than good for kids. It might make them less intrinsically motivated and more scared of making mistakes. Focusing on how much effort they put in is much better! Saying things like "I see you're trying really hard," "You were so patient to do that," or "I like how you're so focused on learning this" can really help kids feel good. The concept of "growth mindset" was developed by Stanford professor Carol Dweck. She stated, "What we've found in study after study is that ability-praise backfires. Emphasizing effort gives a child a variable that they can control. They come to see themselves as in control of their success. Emphasizing natural intelligence takes it out of the child's control, and it provides no good recipe for responding to a failure" (VanDeVelde, 2007).

Play Games That Promote Flexible Thinking

Here are a few fun games to try:

- Coogan Rainbow Puzzle Ball Brain Teaser: Ages 5+
- Gravity Maze Marble Run Brain Game: Ages 8+
- Rush Hour Traffic Jam Logic Puzzle: Ages 8+

- Penguins on Ice—A Sliding Cognitive Skill-Building Puzzle Game: Ages 6+

16. Read Storybooks That Are Fun and Teach Flexible Thinking

Here is a list of some of my favorite books to read:

- *The Dot* by Peter H. Reynolds
- *Evelyn Del Rey Is Moving Away* by Meg Medina
- *Florette* by Anna Walker
- *Home is a Window* by Stephanie Ledyard
- *A Home for Gully* by Jo Clegg
- *The Koala Who Could* by Rachel Bright
- *One Word from Sophia* by Jim Averbeck
- *Perfect Square* by Michael Hall
- *The Quiet Place* by Sarah Stewart
- *Ruby Finds a Worry* by Tom Percival
- *Saturday* by Oge Mora
- *Stuck* by Oliver Jeffers
- *After the Fall* by Dan Santat
- *My Day is Ruined* by Bryan Smith
- *Flexible Thinking Ninja* by Mary Nhin
- *Beautiful Oops* by Barney Saltzberg
- *She Persisted* by Chelsea Clinton
- *Flight School* by Lita Judge
- *The Most Magnificent Thing* by Ashley Spires
- *Your Fantastic Elastic Brain* by JoAnn Deak, Ph.D
- *The Magical Yet* by Angela DiTerlizzi

CONCLUSION

Embracing and fostering adaptable thinking in children is paramount for their holistic development. Ben's journey vividly illustrates the struggles that can arise when routine is disrupted, emphasizing the need to teach adaptable thinking skills explicitly. As we navigate a world filled with uncertainties and unexpected changes, the ability to approach challenges with flexibility becomes a vital life skill.

The strategies in this chapter offer practical ways to empower children to develop adaptable thinking. From teaching language rules and problem-solving skills to validating emotions and modeling flexibility, these approaches aim to equip children with the tools to navigate life's twists and turns successfully. Recognizing the signs of struggle and intervening with understanding and support can significantly affect a child's ability to adapt and thrive.

Ultimately, adaptable thinking is not just a skill; it's a mindset that opens doors to improved learning, enhanced social interactions, and better mental health outcomes. As we guide our children through the process of understanding and embracing adaptable thinking, we contribute to their immediate well-being and their lifelong capacity for resilience and success in an ever-changing world. Let's keep going and learn all about our next super skill, planning and prioritizing!

SUPER SKILL #4: PLANNING AND PRIORITIZING

"If you fail to plan, you are planning to fail!"

— BENJAMIN FRANKLIN

In our journey alongside Ben, a sixth grader with executive function challenges, we've witnessed his daily struggles with self-control, flexible thinking, and getting things done. Now, we begin a new chapter in his life, where he discovers the transformative power of planning and prioritizing.

BEN'S STRUGGLES WITH PLANNING

It's 8 p.m., and Ben finally settles in for the night and attempts to begin his homework. Instead of starting his book report or completing his math problems that are due tomorrow, he begins searching online for a science fair topic that is due next week. After several minutes of surfing the web for a topic, he decides to take a break and play a video game. When Ben finally starts his book report, he can't focus. His thoughts keep jumping around, and he doesn't know what to write. He only manages to write one sentence before giving up for the night. He thinks he'll just finish writing it on the bus to school tomorrow, even though he's never been able to finish work while chatting with his friends. This shows how hard it can be for kids like Ben to plan and decide what's most important. In this chapter, we'll talk about why planning and prioritizing are so important and share some tips to help kids like Ben get better at it.

PLANNING AT A GLANCE

Planning is the art of envisioning your day, and goals, and then charting the course to reach them. It's the skill that allows individuals to navigate their days with purpose, structure, and efficiency. For children like Ben, who often find themselves lost in a sea of disorganization, planning is the lighthouse guiding them toward smoother, less stressful days.

At its core, planning involves thinking ahead, strategizing, and deciding what needs to get done, how it should get done, and when it should be completed. It's the blueprint that helps children set the course for their day, just as a roadmap guides travelers to their destination. Imagine your child's day as a journey. Without a plan, it's easy to get lost or feel overwhelmed by the twists and turns. In this context, planning serves as a detailed guide that outlines the route, highlights potential obstacles, and suggests the best path to reach the destination.

Planning empowers children to make informed decisions about their tasks, priorities, and time management. It helps them anticipate challenges, prepare solutions, and confidently navigate their day.

PRIORITIZATION AT A GLANCE

Prioritization is a skill that can empower children to manage their time more effectively and make consistent progress toward their goals. In a nutshell, prioritizing is the ability to determine the order in which tasks should be completed based on their importance. It also means making sure priorities are aligned with goals and responsibilities. Planning and prioritizing are essential executive function skills for children to learn for the following reasons:

1. Reduces Stress

When children learn to plan, they can avoid last-minute rushes and reduce stress. Ben's frantic morning routines and the anxiety he experiences from forgetting important items could have been minimized through effective planning.

2. Enhances Organization

Planning promotes organization, ensuring children have everything they need for various activities throughout the day. This skill would have been especially beneficial for Ben in helping him remember to pack his lunch or gym clothes.

3. Builds Independence

As children become proficient planners, they gain a sense of independence and self-reliance. They can take charge of their responsibilities and tasks, fostering a sense of empowerment.

4. Helps Kids Achieve Goals

Planning is the bridge that connects goals to reality. Children can make their dreams more achievable by setting clear goals and planning how to achieve them. Whether it's acing a test or excelling in extracurricular activities, planning is the key to progress.

5. Assists Kids with Initiating Tasks and Following Through to Complete Projects

Planning can make beginning a non-preferred task easier by helping kids see a beginning and ending point. For example, when starting a chore, plan to work on it for ten minutes and then prepare for a break. Include an ending time so kids can see that their task won't last forever and that there is an end in sight.

HOW TO SPOT IF A CHILD IS HAVING TROUBLE WITH PLANNING AND PRIORITIZING

Let's look at some of the behaviors you might notice in a child who is struggling with planning and prioritizing skills:

- Tends to complete unimportant tasks before essential tasks and fails to identify the difference between the two
- Feels overwhelmed trying to get chores or homework completed
- Has trouble making goals even in areas they are interested in
- Gets caught up in the little details and struggles to see the big picture
- Has difficulty keeping belongings organized

- Holds on to everything rather than deciding which items to keep and which items they can throw away
- Has difficulty making decisions
- Struggles to anticipate the consequences of their actions
- Easily distracted or forgetful
- Frequently missing the right materials at the right time, including leaving home without all the required items or leaving behind personal belongings at school or a friend's house
- May do tasks quickly and carelessly or slowly and incomplete
- Difficulties thinking or doing more than one thing at a time
- Has a hard time with surprises or unexpected problems
- Takes longer than others to change from one activity to another
- Procrastinates frequently
- Struggles with task initiation

If you see some of these behaviors in your child, it could mean that they would benefit from some executive functioning support in this area. Planning and prioritizing skills can be difficult for even adults to become proficient in, so it's important to give our kids lots of practice and patience when developing these skills. Let's learn some great ways we can help our kids work on these critical skills.

STRATEGIES FOR DEVELOPING PLANNING SKILLS IN CHILDREN

Planning and prioritizing skills can be taught through intentional, concrete instruction and are important in various areas of a child's life. These skills can help kids organize their activities, such as completing homework, watching TV, and finishing chores. At school, planning is essential for completing classwork and having all the materials you need to have a successful day. To teach these skills effectively, parents and educators can start with these four strategies that can positively impact children's academic and personal lives. These strategies can help improve a child's ability to plan and prioritize effectively.

1. Help Children Understand That Planning Is a Crucial Part of Doing and Can Save Time

It is essential to teach children that planning ensures that important aspects of a task are not missed and to show them that planning can make things easier by breaking activities into manageable parts. This will help children feel less overwhelmed and more in control of their workload.

2. Teach Children How to Use Visual Reminders as a Planning Tool

Parents and educators can use visual aids to help kids remember important tasks and the materials that are needed to complete each activity. For example, early childhood teachers can post pictures of the items students need to complete an assignment, such as pictures of scissors, glue, crayons, and a pencil. Students can refer to these visuals as they work on the activity. Teaching older students to use calendars and planners can be valuable visual tools to support planning. Parents and educators should give support by providing reminders as needed.

3. Prompt Children to Verbalize What Success Looks Like Before Starting a Project or Task

Knowing what you're planning for is necessary for a positive outcome. It's helpful to ask your child questions such as, "What materials do you need to get started?" or "What are the steps you think you need to do to accomplish this task?" This is a great way to help your child begin to plan out the steps needed to complete the activity successfully. When possible, provide a finished sample of an activity as a model.

4. Involve Children in Family Planning

Spend about fifteen minutes a day creating a daily planning routine with your child. This will help children get into the habit of practicing these skills each day. Setting up a shared family calendar will help children see the week ahead and learn planning and prioritizing skills. Encourage them to add their activities to the calendar, too. For example, children can plan a sleepover with their friends and decide what activities the friend group will do and how they will get set up.

THE RELATIONSHIP BETWEEN TIME AND PLANNING

In the intricate dance of daily life, planning and time management waltz together. They are inseparable partners, and their coordination can lead to smooth, productive days. For children like Ben, understanding this relationship is pivotal in avoiding the turmoil that results from poor time management.

There are three big ideas to consider when teaching kids about planning and time management. First, it's important to understand that planning involves looking ahead and deciding how to structure your day or allocate your resources. It's about thinking through what needs to be done and how long each task might take. Without this anticipatory step, time can slip away unnoticed. Second, there are consequences for having poor time management. Ben's missed bus incidents are stark examples of this. When children don't manage their time effectively, they often rush, become stressed, and face the fallout of disorganization. And lastly, it's important to point out that time is a finite resource. There are only twenty-four hours in a day, and how you choose to allocate those hours can significantly impact productivity and well-being. Effective planning helps make the most of this valuable resource.

ESTIMATING TASK DURATION

For many children, accurately estimating how much time tasks will take can be challenging. They may underestimate the time needed for homework, projects, or even daily routines, which can lead to time management problems and increased stress.

TIPS FOR TEACHING TIME ESTIMATION

1. Break Tasks into Smaller Steps

Encourage children to break large tasks into smaller, more manageable steps. This makes estimating the time required for each component easier and ensures they don't overlook important details.

2. Use Timers and Clocks

Introduce timers or clocks to help children grasp the concept of time more concretely. For instance, if a math assignment typically takes twenty minutes, setting a timer can visually represent that duration. I love to use visual timers in my classroom as a fun way to help kids "see" time moving. There are many excellent timers available on Amazon! I use the *Secura 60-Minute Visual Timer Countdown Timer for Kids and Adults* in my classroom. My students really respond to the timers and have learned that they need to follow these three steps to complete their work in the time allotted:

1. Get started right away
2. Work the whole time
3. Work quietly

3. Reflect and Adjust

After completing tasks, encourage children to reflect on how long it actually took compared to their initial estimate. This practice helps them refine their time estimation skills over time.

4. Prioritize Tasks by Time

As children prioritize their tasks, they should consider how much time each one will consume. This allows them to allocate their time more effectively and avoid overcommitting.

TIPS FOR ALLOCATING TIME WISELY

1. Use a Planner

Utilizing a planner or digital calendar can be a valuable tool for time management. Planners and apps can help children allocate time for each task, ensuring a balanced schedule. Here are a few good apps to try:

- MyHomework: A student planner that helps keep track of homework and other assignments
- 2Do: This is a planning app for project and task management
- Mind Map: An app that connects ideas to create graphic organizers
- To-Do Reminder: Create simple to-do lists and reminders

2. Prioritize Important Tasks

Help guide your child to identify important and urgent tasks. This will ensure they receive the appropriate amount of time in the schedule and will prevent last-minute rushes.

By teaching children the relationship between planning and time management, we equip them with essential skills that can enhance their productivity and reduce the stress caused by poor time management.

THE IMPORTANCE OF ADAPTABILITY

Imagine planning as a journey and flexibility as the navigator who helps us manage detours and unexpected turns along the way. While planning is essential, it's equally important to teach children that life is inherently unpredictable. Unexpected events, disruptions, or new opportunities can arise at any moment, altering the course of our plans. Teaching children that plans can change due to these unforeseen circumstances is a crucial life lesson. For kids like Ben, who may be prone to frustration when faced with changes, mastering this skill can make their journey smoother.

TEACHING ADAPTATION

1. Problem-Solving Skills

Teach children how to approach unexpected changes as problems to be solved. Encourage them to think critically and creatively to find alternative solutions when plans need to change.

2. Emotional Regulation

Children may feel frustrated or anxious when plans change. Help them develop emotional regulation skills, such as deep breathing or positive self-talk, to manage their reactions constructively.

3. Flexibility Exercises

Engage children in flexibility exercises by intentionally altering plans from time to time in a controlled environment. This helps them practice adapting and builds confidence in their ability to handle change.

4. Highlight Opportunities

Teach children to view changes in plans as opportunities for growth and learning. Sometimes, a change can lead to new experiences or insights they wouldn't have encountered otherwise.

5. Role Modeling

As parents and teachers, model adaptability in your own life. Share stories of how you adapted to changes in your plans and the positive outcomes that resulted.

6. Emphasize Resilience

Remind children that being resilient in the face of change is a valuable life skill. Resilience helps individuals bounce back from setbacks and continue moving forward.

7. Encourage Open Communication

Create an environment where children feel comfortable discussing changes in plans or any challenges they face. Open communication fosters adaptability.

8. Practice, Practice, Practice

Give plenty of opportunities to practice these skills.

10. Mock Scenarios

Create hypothetical scenarios where plans need to change and involve children in brainstorming solutions. This practice can help them feel more prepared when real changes occur.

11. Review and Reflect

After a change in plans, encourage children to reflect on what they learned from the experience. This reinforces the idea that adaptation can lead to personal growth.

By instilling the importance of adaptability within planning and teaching children how to navigate changes with a positive mindset, we as parents and teachers can equip them with valuable life skills that not only enhance their academic performance but also help them become more resilient, self-assured, and better prepared to handle the unpredictable nature of life.

STRATEGIES FOR DEVELOPING PRIORITIZATION SKILLS

Have you ever stared at a long to-do list that left you feeling overwhelmed and unsure where to even start? You're not alone. Many adults struggle with prioritization, and it can feel even more overwhelming for children. Fortunately, it's a skill that can be introduced at an early age. Whether you're a parent hoping to instill a better sense of prioritization in your child or a teacher who wants to implement these skills across the entire classroom, you can follow these simple strategies:

1. Teach Task Priority

In the grand scheme of a day filled with responsibilities and activities, not all tasks hold the same weight. Understanding task priority is the first step toward effective planning and time management. Learning this skill is transformative for children like Ben, who often feel overwhelmed by the sheer volume of things they need to accomplish.

Importance vs. Urgency: It's crucial to convey to children that tasks can be divided into two key categories: importance and urgency. While some tasks are both important and urgent, others may be important but not necessarily urgent, or vice versa. Understanding this distinction is fundamental to making informed choices about how to allocate time and effort.

- **Importance:** Tasks deemed necessary are those that align with a child's goals, values, and priorities. For example, completing homework assignments, preparing for exams, or participating in extracurricular activities may fall under the category of important tasks. These activities contribute directly to a child's growth and development.
- **Urgency:** Urgent tasks are those with impending deadlines or time-sensitive requirements. Examples include meeting a project deadline, responding to immediate requests, or addressing critical responsibilities like medical appointments. Urgency often drives the need for quick action.

2. Identify Priorities

An important step in teaching prioritization is helping children identify their priorities. Encourage them to reflect on their goals and responsibilities. Ask questions like, "What do you want to accomplish today?" or "What are your most important tasks this week?" This introspection helps children clearly understand what matters most to them.

3. Teach the Eisenhower Matrix

The Eisenhower Matrix is a simple but powerful tool that categorizes tasks into four quadrants based on their importance and urgency. Older children can use this matrix to determine which tasks require immediate attention, which can be scheduled, and which may be delegated or postponed. For example:

- **Quadrant 1 (Urgent and Important):** These tasks demand immediate attention and should be top priorities.
- **Quadrant 2 (Not Urgent but Important):** These tasks contribute to long-term goals and require proactive planning.
- **Quadrant 3 (Urgent but Not Important):** Tasks in this quadrant may be delegated or streamlined to reduce time spent on them.
- **Quadrant 4 (Not Urgent and Not Important):** These tasks can often be eliminated or postponed.

Example of the Eisenhower Matrix

	URGENT	NOT URGENT
IMPORTANT	1. Do First	2. Schedule
NOT IMPORTANT	3. Delegate	4. Delete

For younger children, you can start by using words like "have to" and "want to." Ask your child questions such as "What is something we have to do today?" Examples could include brushing teeth, getting dressed, or finishing a homework assignment. Then, ask them to identify things that they want to do today. This could be things like playing with toys or going on a bike ride. Then, help them rank these activities using a 1-2-3 system. Start with the "have to" activities and end with the want to activities. For example:

1. Brush teeth
2. Complete schoolwork
3. Play with toys

This is a simple way of helping kids begin to understand how to prioritize activities.

4. Use Real-Life Examples of Task Prioritization

Share real-life scenarios and examples with children to illustrate the concept of task prioritization. For instance, you can discuss how preparing for a school project (important) should take precedence over watching TV (not urgent or important) when deadlines are approaching. Starting with tasks kids are familiar with can also help introduce the concept of planning and prioritizing. For example, you could start by helping your child plan out the steps needed to make their bed. Help them identify the necessary steps and then determine when they should do this each day.

5. Create a Prioritized To-Do List

Encourage children to create a to-do list that reflects their priorities. This list should include tasks ranked by importance and urgency. By visually organizing their tasks, children can understand what needs immediate attention and what can wait. Try writing to-do items on colorful sticky notes. This way, your child can peel off the notes as they complete each task.

Encourage kids to create their to-do lists with input from both home and school. This collaborative approach ensures that responsibilities from both environments are considered.

THE ROLE OF PARENTS AND TEACHERS

Effective planning and prioritizing skills are not innate but nurtured through guidance and support from home and school environments. Parents and teachers play pivotal roles in helping children develop these essential life skills. In this section, we'll explore how parents and teachers can collaborate to empower children like Ben.

HOW PARENTS CAN SUPPORT PLANNING AND PRIORITIZING SKILLS

1. Create a Structured Home Environment

Establishing a structured and organized home environment can set the stage for effective planning. Designate specific areas for homework and playing. Ensure that school supplies are readily accessible.

2. Set Clear Expectations

Communicate clear expectations to your child regarding responsibilities and tasks. Whatever strategies you decide to try with your child (to-do lists, planners, etc.), be consistent and check in with them often to see how they are doing.

3. Create Routines

- **Consistent Schedules:** Work with your children to establish consistent daily schedules. This includes setting regular times for sleeping, eating, studying, completing chores, and leisure time activities. These routines will help create a predictable daily plan.
- **Discuss Daily Plans:** Take some time each day to talk about how the day will go, either at breakfast or on the way to school.
- **Get Things Ready the Night Before:** Encourage kids to gather school materials and clothes for the next day the night before. This is a huge time saver for busy mornings and is a good routine to develop.
- **Routine Review:** Periodically review routines with children to ensure they are effective and address any necessary adjustments or changes.

4. Choose a Recipe Together and Plan Out How to Make It

Cooking always requires planning and is a fun way to help kids begin to understand the planning process. Before starting, make a list of all the ingredients needed together and have your child help gather everything.

5. Offer Encouragement

Provide positive reinforcement when your kids exhibit effective planning and prioritizing behaviors. Praise their efforts and celebrate their achievements.

This positive reinforcement can boost their motivation to continue developing these skills. Understand that developing these skills may take time. Offer consistent support and patience, reassuring them that their efforts are valued. Providing your children with practical guidance and support creates a cohesive environment that reinforces planning and prioritizing skills. This partnership empowers them to excel academically and thrive personally and socially.

6. Constructive Feedback

When children face challenges in planning or prioritizing, offer constructive feedback rather than criticism. Encourage them to learn from mistakes and make improvements.

7. Model Planning and Prioritization

Children learn by example. Demonstrate effective planning and prioritizing in your daily life. Share your own experiences and strategies for managing time and responsibilities.

HOW TEACHERS CAN SUPPORT PLANNING AND PRIORITIZING SKILLS

1. Create Structured Routines

Implement structured routines within the classroom, including designated times for assignments, breaks, and transitions. Start each day with a morning meeting that outlines the day's schedule. Create a visual schedule by adding pictures and times for each subject/activity for students to refer to throughout the day. Routines provide a predictable framework for students.

2. Regular Check-Ins

Conduct regular check-ins with students to discuss their planning and prioritizing efforts. Offer constructive feedback and guidance based on individual needs.

3. Teach Planning Techniques

Dedicate classroom time to teach planning techniques, such as goal setting, creating to-do lists, and using time management tools like planners and visual timers.

4. Collaborate with Parents

Maintain open lines of communication with parents regarding students' planning and prioritizing progress. Discuss strategies that can be reinforced both at home and in school.

FUN STRATEGY GAMES TO PROMOTE PLANNING AND PRIORITIZING

- Ticket to Ride: Ages 8+
- Magic Labyrinth: Ages 6+
- Jump In: Ages 7+
- Cribbage: Ages 7+
- Codenames: Ages 10+
- Scrabble: Ages 8+
- Scrabble Junior: Ages 5+
- 5 Second Rule: Ages 10+
- Jenga: Ages 6+
- Storytime Chess: Ages 3+
- Regular Chess: Ages 5+

RECOMMENDED STORY BOOK FOR TEACHING PLANNING AND PRIORITIZING:

- *Planning Isn't My Priority...And Making Priorities Isn't in My Plans* By Julia Cook

CONCLUSION

In this chapter, we explored the super skill of planning and prioritizing. We started by revisiting Ben's challenges, understanding how his difficulties in planning often led to chaotic and stressful days. Through detailed discussions and practical guidance, we uncovered the significance of planning in a child's life and how it can be a powerful tool for success academically, personally, socially, and professionally. We learned several key takeaways:

- **Planning as a Roadmap:** Planning serves as a roadmap for a child's day, helping them make informed choices about tasks, priorities, and time management.
- **Task Priority:** We looked at the concepts of task importance and urgency, teaching children how to distinguish between tasks and prioritize effectively.
- **Time Management:** We learned the interconnection between planning and time management, emphasizing the consequences of poor time management, as seen in Ben's story.
- **Flexibility in Planning:** We also saw the importance of adaptability in planning, explaining that plans can change due to unexpected circumstances. Practical strategies for teaching adaptation and fostering a positive mindset toward changes in plans were provided.
- **Involving Parents and Teachers:** This chapter underlined the pivotal roles of parents and teachers in supporting a child's planning and prioritizing skills. It stressed the importance of collaboration between home and school.

We discussed how improved planning and prioritizing skills can profoundly transform a child's life. By mastering these skills, children can:

- **Reduce Stress:** Effective planning allows children to avoid last-minute rushes, resulting in reduced stress and anxiety.
- **Enhance Organization:** Planning promotes organization, ensuring children have everything they need for various activities throughout the day.
- **Build Independence:** As children become proficient planners, they gain a sense of independence and self-reliance, taking charge of their responsibilities and tasks.

- **Achieve Goals:** Planning acts as a bridge that connects goals to reality. Children can make their dreams more achievable, whether it's excelling academically, personally, or succeeding in their social lives.
- **Foster Resilience:** The ability to adapt plans and navigate changes cultivates resilience, enabling children to bounce back from setbacks and continue progressing.

Now, let's turn our attention to super skill number five—organization!

Super Skills for All Children

"An investment in knowledge pays the best interest."

— BENJAMIN FRANKLIN

As I'm sure you're aware, the majority of materials designed to prepare children for kindergarten and school are heavily focused on academic skills. I agree that there's a place for that, and no child is going to be set back by learning the alphabet or how to count to ten before they set foot in a classroom. Nonetheless, I believe executive functioning skills are far more helpful as a focus for getting children ready for school. They're going to be taught English and math anyway; it's far better to focus on honing the skills they need to function well in the classroom and be ready to receive these lessons.

Parents want to prepare their children for school, and because of the focus on academic skills, this is what many believe will help them the most. With this book, I want to redirect parents and show them the importance of executive functioning skills. If you've ever seen that one kid in your child's classroom, the one labeled "disruptive" or "a handful," you've met a child who was in dire need of these skills, and their parents would probably be more than willing to help—if only they knew how. We can help this information reach more of those parents (as well as the ones who simply want to prepare their children for the world) by spreading the word, and this is where I'd like to ask for your help. If you'd be willing to leave a short review, you'll play an important role in sharing this information.

By leaving a review of this book on Amazon, you'll make it more visible to parents looking for resources to help them prepare their children for the classroom.

Reviews serve to help new readers select the materials that are going to help them the most, and your words will show parents the value of helping children develop their executive functioning skills. It's that easy to spread knowledge.

Thank you so much for your support. We expect a lot from our children when they go to school, and it's important that we help them prepare for it.

Scan the QR code below

SUPER SKILL #5: ORGANIZATION

"Organizing is something you do before you do something so that when you do it, it is not all mixed up."

— A. A. MILNE

In this chapter, we'll examine the fifth super skill: organization. We'll explore how the power of organizing can change the trajectory of a child's day and how it can transform their lives for the better. Organization is the tool we use to bring order to chaos, streamline our lives, and ensure that every activity we begin is not a tangled mess. Organization is the glue that holds everything together in a child's day. It's the skill that helps them arrange their world systematically, keep track of their belongings, and follow a plan. It's not just about keeping things tidy (although that's important); it is about having a well-structured plan for the day.

Think about a typical morning: your child wakes up, gets dressed, has breakfast, and heads to school. Without organization, these simple tasks can turn into a frenzy. Imagine them searching for their school bag when the bus is about to arrive—that's not fun!

Organization is like having a checklist that guides you through each step, making sure you have enough time for everything. It's the reason we can easily find things when we need them. In a nutshell, organization is a necessary skill to develop so our kids can thrive, feel in control, and focus on what really matters—their learning and growth.

BEN'S STRUGGLES WITH ORGANIZATION

Ben's bedroom is always super messy! His parents dread walking in, not knowing what they might step on or what kind of rotting food might be hiding in the chaos! His parents hope that he will eventually get tired of not knowing where his things are or get sick of getting into trouble. But no matter how they try to help Ben get organized, it's always short-lived, and it seems like they are fighting a losing battle. Now imagine a typical morning in Ben's life, around 7 a.m. He's supposed to be heading to meet the school bus. But, more often than not, this moment turns into a mini disaster.

First, there's the moment of realization—Ben has forgotten something. It could be his lunch for the day or his gym clothes. Today, he realizes he doesn't have his gym clothes. He runs back to his room to look for them but can't find them in the heap of clothes piled up on the floor. He yells to his mom, asking her if she knows where his clothes are. She is frustrated, too, because his gym clothes probably never even came back from school, or if they did, they probably didn't make it into the hamper. This situation is like the first domino in a chain reaction of chaos for the day.

But here's the thing: Ben's problems with organization are not unique. Many kids face similar challenges. They forget homework, misplace their school stuff, and feel overwhelmed. Without organization, they, too, might find themselves in a whirlwind of stress, trying to keep up with school and life.

It can be easy for parents and educators to lose patience when children have organizational challenges. It might even feel like these kids are lazy or defiant because even when they are asked to clean up, they often never do. However, many kids like Ben need help with organization and all the skills that go along with it. So do many adults! People struggle with organization for different reasons. As parents and teachers, we can see that Ben's problems with organization are not just about minor inconveniences. They touch every aspect of his life, from his punctuality to his emotional well-being. Helping kids like Ben become more organized can set the stage for better school days and brighter futures.

ORGANIZATION AT A GLANCE

Imagine if our world was without organization—it would be chaotic! Things would be misplaced, tasks would be forgotten, and each day would feel like a puzzle with missing pieces. But when we talk about organization, we're talking about the power to prevent all that chaos. Organization is like the magical thread that weaves order into our daily lives. It's all about arranging things in a thoughtful and tidy way so that everything has its place and purpose. For kids, it's like having a superpower that can make their school days smoother and less stressful. Organization is crucial in our daily routines and tasks.

BENEFITS OF HAVING STRONG ORGANIZATIONAL SKILLS

The impact of organizational skills on a child's life is profound. When children embrace organization, they unlock a world of possibilities and experience the following outcomes:

1. Reduced Stress

Organization empowers children to start their days with confidence and control, reducing stress and anxiety. Picture a child like Ben, who often starts his day in a chaotic rush. When he forgets essential items or tasks due to disorganization, it triggers a whirlwind of stress and anxiety. When a child is stressed, their body goes into a "fight or flight" mode. This can affect their ability to focus, learn, and interact with peers. Stress can be a significant hurdle in a child's educational journey. It can lead to self-doubt, frustration, and even health issues. But here's where organization comes to the rescue. When kids are organized, they reduce the chances of encountering those stressful morning surprises. They know where their belongings are, what tasks they need to complete, and how to manage their time effectively. This sense of control significantly lowers their stress levels and allows them to approach their day with confidence and calm.

2. Effective Time Management

Time is a precious resource, especially for children juggling school, homework, extracurricular activities, and playtime. Without organization, time can slip through their fingers like grains of sand. When kids are organized, they gain the ability to allocate their time wisely. They learn how to plan their day, setting aside dedicated slots for different tasks. This skill helps them avoid the last-minute rush and the stress accompanying it. Instead, they can complete their assignments, projects, and chores more efficiently. Think about Ben's mornings again. When disorganized, he loses precious time racing back home to fetch forgotten items. That time could have been better spent preparing for the day ahead. Organization empowers kids to make the most of their time, allowing them to focus on their studies and enjoy the benefits of a well-balanced life.

3. Responsibility and Independence

Responsibility is like a seed that when cultivated, blossoms into a lifelong attribute. When kids learn to be organized, they take ownership of their belongings and tasks. They become more self-reliant and dependable. This benefits them not only in school but also in their relationships and future careers.

Consider Ben's experiences. When he forgets his lunch, he realizes the importance of being responsible for his own needs. Parents and teachers can use these moments to help children connect the dots between organization and responsibility. When they understand that being organized is a way of taking care of themselves and their responsibilities, they're more likely to embrace this super skill.

4. Confidence and Resilience

Through organization, children gain the confidence to face challenges, learn from their mistakes, and develop resilience.

5. Success in School and Beyond

As children become more organized, they are better prepared to succeed in school and their future endeavors.

THE ROLE OF PROBLEM-SOLVING AND RESILIENCE IN DEVELOPING ORGANIZATION SKILLS

Problem-solving and resilience are two essential qualities that go hand in hand with developing organizational skills. When children face organizational challenges, they need to think critically about solutions. Encourage them to brainstorm ideas and consider different approaches to tackle their issues. Resilience is the ability to bounce back from setbacks and keep moving forward. As children encounter difficulties in organizing their tasks or materials, help them develop resilience by emphasizing that mistakes are opportunities to grow stronger. Teach them strategies to overcome obstacles and stay motivated on their organizational journey.

Embracing patience and persistence is fundamental when teaching organizational skills to children. Remember that it's a gradual process, and setbacks are part of the learning experience. Kids also benefit the most when parents and teachers work together to help them develop these skills. If you notice your child is struggling with these skills, do not hesitate to set up a meeting with their teacher. It's important to share what you are noticing and for the teacher to know what strategies you are trying at home. This way, the teacher can be on the same page and provide the same support at school.

WHY ORGANIZATION MATTERS FOR SCHOOL LEARNING

When kids struggle with organizational skills, opening their backpacks can be a terrifying experience. Crumpled-up assignments and tests, school announcements from two weeks ago, even smelly gym clothes—it's a disaster!

Many people think of organizational skills as the ability to keep *things* in order. However, we also use these skills to keep our *thoughts* in order to retrieve and use information effectively.

Children who struggle with organization often find it hard to manage information in a smart and sensible manner. They might have trouble deciding what's most important, making plans, staying focused, and finishing tasks. These abilities become more and more important as kids go through school. The good news is that children can learn these skills through practice. And being organized can help them feel less stressed, manage their time better, and finish their work faster.

Developing organizational and planning skills in early childhood is essential because good organization skills help create ready learners, leading to intelligent and successful students. Children who learn good organization skills in their early years are more likely to maintain these skills throughout their lives and lead a cleaner, happier, and healthier lifestyle as they grow up. Good organization skills help kids create a plan and follow through with it, enabling them to complete their work efficiently. They can plan steps to complete a task and easily follow directions, leading to better focus.

FOUR WAYS KIDS USE ORGANIZATIONAL SKILLS TO LEARN

1. Organization and Following Directions

Following directions requires children to engage in two key activities: concentrating on the task at hand and developing a strategy to accomplish it. Both activities use mental organization and planning. Students with strong organizational skills can often follow directions effortlessly. They can plan out the steps needed to get something done. However, when kids have organizational challenges, they may not be able to see the necessary sequence of steps contained in directions or even know where to start.

2. Organization and Learning to Read

When kids begin to learn how to read, they use organization skills in small ways. Think of it like this: imagine that kids have a mental filing system in their brain where they store uppercase and lowercase letters together with the sound (or sounds) that letter makes. The process of learning involves establishing connections between sounds and letters. When encountering a letter, they can retrieve the associated sound from their mental filing system. As children progress to reading sight words, the complexity of their filing system increases. Sight words are common words that children learn to recognize visually. They must match the visual appearance of the word with its corresponding sound and meaning. If kids have difficulty staying organized, they might find it challenging to remember the information they need to match letters with their sounds and figure out what groups of letters mean.

3. Organization and Literacy Learning

Learning to read, write, and understand grammar—what we call literacy—needs good organization. When kids read books or write, they need to remember lots of things: who the characters are, what happens in the story, the order of events, important details, and what the main point is. If they're reading nonfiction, they must also remember unique words about the topic. Kids who find it hard to stay organized might struggle to organize all this information and put it in order. And if they need to keep stopping to look up words while reading, they might lose track of what's happening in the story.

4. Organization and Learning Math

Children need to use organizational skills to grasp the rules and procedures of mathematics. Math involves arranging information according to relationships, such as sorting items into groups based on size, shape, or color. As mathematical concepts become more abstract, the ability to establish mental categories for organizing information becomes increasingly challenging. Additionally, organizational skills are crucial for deciphering word problems that involve clue words, such as interpreting "fewer than" as subtraction. For children facing difficulties with organization, storing, and recalling rules and facts in math can prove to be super challenging.

HOW TO SPOT ORGANIZATIONAL CHALLENGES IN CHILDREN

Some signs of organization problems are easy to see, like a messy bedroom. But there are other signs that are not as obvious. Here are some examples:

- Forgetting to bring important things to and from school, like homework
- Not getting all the right stuff together for a task or project
- Not putting things in the same place all the time, so it's hard to find them
- Finding it hard to think about or do more than one thing at once
- Having trouble telling a story in a way that makes sense

STRATEGIES FOR TEACHING ORGANIZATION

Checklists: Your Roadmap to Organization

One of the most effective tools for teaching organization is the humble checklist. It's like a roadmap for kids, guiding them through their tasks and responsibilities. Create daily or weekly checklists that outline what needs to be done. Encourage kids to check off each item as they complete it. This simple act gives them a sense of accomplishment and helps them stay on track. I found an awesome chore chart that has sliding windows for each chore. It allows kids to close the window after they complete each chore. This is an excellent way for kids to keep track of their daily chores and is a visual reminder of what tasks they still need to finish. This chart is available on Amazon and is called the *Dry Erase Chore Chart for Kids, Reusable Checklist Board Tools for Kids, To-Do List Daily Routine.*

Establishing Routines: Consistency is Key

Kids thrive on routines. Establish consistent schedules for mornings and evenings. A predictable routine helps children know what to expect, reducing anxiety and making them more receptive to organization. For example, a morning routine might include waking up, going to the bathroom, getting dressed, having breakfast, brushing teeth, and going over their checklist before heading out to school.

Visual Aids: Charts, Calendars, and More

Visual aids are invaluable tools for teaching organization. Create charts that illustrate tasks and responsibilities. Use wall calendars to track important dates like project due dates and school events. Visual aids make abstract concepts concrete for kids. They can see their progress and plan ahead more effectively.

Decluttering: A Lesson in Simplicity

Teach children the importance of a clutter-free living space. Explain that a tidy environment makes it easier to find things and reduces distractions. Set aside time for regular decluttering sessions where kids clean up and organize their belongings. Having different-colored bins to collect toys and games can make it easier for kids to know where items belong. Add a picture of what gets stored in each bin to make it even easier to clean up. Use an art caddy to store colored pencils, markers, crayons, and glue. Make sure everything has a designated "home," and it will be easier to always know where to find needed items and keep things tidy at the same time. Remember to make it fun and praise your kids for their efforts.

I recently learned the saying: "Keep up so you don't have to catch up." I love this because it reminds me that staying on top of keeping my things organized is much easier than letting things go for a long time and then having much more work to do to get things back in order. Another trick I recently learned is the "20–

30 step rule." This rule states that you are usually only twenty to thirty steps away from putting an item back where it belongs. This rule always pops into my head when I am about to throw something on the table or counter instead of putting it where it belongs. When I struggle to put something away, I literally count the steps from where I am to where I need to go to put the item away. It really is almost always only twenty to thirty steps away! These little tricks can be helpful to introduce to our kids at a young age, so they learn organizational skills from the very beginning.

Modeling Behavior: Be the Example

Children often learn by watching adults. Be a role model for organization. Show them how you manage your tasks and belongings. Talk them through your thought process when you create checklists or use visual aids. Let them see that organization is a lifelong skill that benefits everyone.

Use a Color-Coding System: A School Work Helper

For older children, color-coding their school supplies can be a huge help. Here are a few tips:

- **Color Code Notebooks by Class Subject:** Choose a different color for each subject. Buy a small notebook in each color and have your child label them with the correct subject.
- **Take Notes Using Different Colors:** Have your child choose two different-colored pens to take notes with at home and school. This way, your child can tell if what they wrote was something the teacher said at school or if it was something they wrote down at home.

- **Buy Different-Colored Drawstring Bags for School Activities:** For example, a red bag for gym clothes and a white bag for soccer gear. Be sure to label each bag with the correct activity. This will create a beneficial grab-and-go system for your child.

Use Inexpensive Rubber Bracelet Bands as Homework Reminders: Get some different-colored rubber bracelet bands to match the colors you used for each subject. Have your child wear or attach the bracelets to their backpack using a carabiner clip. After they complete a homework assignment in a class, they can remove the colored bracelet that matches that class. They could also remove a bracelet if they were not assigned homework in a class. This is a great visual reminder of the work they need to complete at home.

Invest in an Expanding File Organizer: Color code the sections to match your child's classes. Encourage your child to file important papers from class in the correct colored section.

Use a Multi-Compartment Backpack: A sturdy backpack can help kids keep school supplies in order. Look for a multi-compartment backpack with two to three large pockets—one for books, one for notebooks, and one for personal items. The zippered pockets can hold smaller school supplies.

A FEW MORE THOUGHTS ON ORGANIZATION

1. Encouraging Independence

It's important to foster independence in a child's organizational efforts.

Teaching organization is not just about giving kids a set of rules to follow; it's about empowering them to take charge of their own lives. As parents and teachers, our role is to nurture their independence. We do this by gradually entrusting them with more responsibilities related to organization. For parents, it might mean allowing their child to take the lead in preparing their school bag or packing their lunch. For teachers, it involves creating an environment where students have opportunities to make choices and decisions about their assignments and classroom materials.

2. Allowing Children to Take Initiative and Make Decisions

One of the most effective ways to foster independence is by allowing children to take the initiative and make organizational decisions. Encourage them to plan their day, set priorities, and think about how to accomplish their tasks. When children have a say in their routines and organizational strategies, they are more likely to embrace these skills willingly. For example, you can ask your child what they think should be on their daily checklist or let them choose the order in which they complete tasks. In the classroom, give students options for organizing their study materials or managing their time for assignments.

3. Gradually Transfer Responsibility from Adults to Children

As children grow, the goal is to slowly transfer more responsibility for organization from adults to children. This process takes time, and matching the level of responsibility to the child's age and maturity is essential. Parents can start by providing guidance and support but gradually allow their children to take the lead in organizing their school materials, managing their time, and planning their routines. Teachers can scaffold the development of organizational skills by providing structure and eventually giving students more autonomy. It's also helpful to give students time in their daily schedules to organize their materials and desks. Fostering independence and allowing children to make decisions empowers them to actively participate in their own organizational journey. This not only strengthens their organizational skills but also boosts their self-esteem and confidence, setting the stage for success in school and life.

4. Embrace Patience and Understanding in the Learning Process

Teaching organization to children is filled with valuable lessons, and it's best to approach it with patience and understanding. Parents and teachers need to remember that children are still developing these skills and may not get everything right from the start. Be patient and empathetic as they navigate the challenges of becoming more organized. When children make mistakes or encounter setbacks in their organizational efforts, we need to resist the urge to become frustrated or critical. Instead, offer a supportive and understanding presence. Remember to comment on the situation and not on your child personally. For example, instead of saying, "You are so messy!" say things like, "This desk is so messy!" instead. If you find that they haven't cleaned up or have lost something again, say nothing for five seconds. Remind yourself they're not doing it on purpose. Let them know it's okay to make mistakes and that learning organization is a process. Your patience creates a safe environment for them to explore and improve their organizational skills.

5. Teaching Children to Learn from Mistakes and Setbacks

Mistakes and setbacks are valuable teachers on the path to organization. Encourage children to reflect on what went wrong when things don't go as planned. Help them see that mistakes are opportunities for growth and learning. Ask open-ended questions like, "What could you do differently next time?" This fosters problem-solving skills and resilience. Teach children that even when they encounter challenges or forget tasks, it doesn't define their abilities. It's all part of the journey. Emphasize that setbacks are not roadblocks but detours on the way to becoming more organized. By learning from their mistakes, children develop the ability to adapt and improve.

CHILDREN'S BOOKS ABOUT ORGANIZATION THAT ARE FUN TO READ

1. *The Berenstain Bears and the Messy Room* by Stan and Jan Berenstain
2. *Just a Mess (Little Critter)* by Mercer Mayer
3. *Cami Kangaroo Has Too Much Stuff* by Stacy Bauer
4. *Too Many Toys* by David Shannon
5. *Fancy Nancy Too Many Tutus* by Jane O'Connor
6. *Franklin Is Messy* by Paulette Bourgeois
7. *A Place for Everything* by Sean Covey
8. *Clean Up Time* by Elizabeth Yerdick
9. *The Big Tidy* by Norah Smaridge
10. *Grey Rabbit Odd One Out* by Alan Baker
11. *How Do Dinosaurs Clean Their Rooms* by Jane Yolen

CONCLUSION

In this chapter, we explored the super skill of organization and its significance in a child's life. Let's recap the key points and reflect on the potential impact of organizational skills on a child's journey.

- **Understanding Organization:** We looked at the meaning of organization and how it's not just about tidying up but creating order in every aspect of a child's day.
- **Why Organization Matters:** We explored how organization reduces stress, improves time management, and fosters responsibility, all of which are essential for a child's success.
- **Teaching Organization:** Practical strategies like checklists, routines, visual aids, decluttering, and modeling behavior were presented to help guide children toward organization.
- **Encouraging Independence:** We looked at the importance of nurturing independence, allowing children to make decisions, and gradually transferring responsibility to them.
- **Patience and Persistence:** Learning organization is a journey that requires patience, understanding, and the ability to learn from mistakes while building problem-solving skills and resilience.

Now that we understand how vital organizational skills are, let's dive right into super skill number six: time management!

SUPER SKILL #6: TIME MANAGEMENT

"The bad news is time flies. The good news is you're the pilot."

— MICHAEL ALTSHULER

"What are you doing? You're supposed to be getting ready for bed!" Does this sound familiar? We ask our kids to do something only to check on them a few minutes later and find that they haven't even started on what we asked them to do. No matter the chore or task, it can be a real challenge to get them to do even simple things independently. While it can be very frustrating when this happens, it's important to remember that our kids are not being lazy or disobedient. It may mean that they need help with time management, which, like any other life skill, is something parents and educators need to teach. Time management is a critical executive function skill. But what exactly is the skill of time management? Let's revisit our student, Ben, this time focusing on his daily struggle with time management. This recap will highlight his frantic mornings and how his difficulties with managing time affect his entire day, providing valuable insights for parents and teachers working with children.

BEN'S STRUGGLES WITH TIME MANAGEMENT

Every morning around 7 a.m., Ben starts his race against the clock. It's a race he often loses. Today, he slept through his alarm! It's probably because he stayed up way too late trying to finish his homework. He thought he had plenty of time to finish his assignments before bedtime, so he took a lot of breaks throughout the night to play some video games. His homework was taking a lot longer than he thought it would, and before he knew it, it was way past his bedtime! His mom tried waking him up several times this morning, and now she is frustrated that he still hasn't gotten up. She begins yelling at him to get dressed quickly and come downstairs to eat breakfast! He is rushing around his room trying to find his soccer uniform when he suddenly remembers he needs to bring a book to school for *drop everything and read time*! Ben flings items from his bookshelf, desperately trying to find a book. He is now so late for school that his mom comes storming up the stairs to tell him he has missed the bus again! She is upset that she will be late for work because she has to drive Ben to school! The consequences of these chaotic mornings are far-reaching. One of the most immediate impacts is that Ben misses the school bus. This sets a stressful tone for his day, and he feels the weight of his time-related issues. Being late for school makes him anxious, and he constantly worries that he might have forgotten something else.

TIME MANAGEMENT AT A GLANCE

Time management is the art of using time wisely to achieve goals, stay organized, and reduce stress. It also includes an awareness that time matters.

Kids who have trouble managing their time might find that their plans don't work out like they hoped. They often need to catch up and figure out how to fit everything in. In this chapter, we'll explore ways you can help your child strengthen this skill. Just like any other skill, time management can be improved with clear instructions and practice.

THE IMPORTANCE OF TIME MANAGEMENT

Time management is a valuable executive function skill for children, as it enables them to prioritize their tasks and complete them promptly. This skill involves managing and planning how much time to spend on different activities, evaluating the time required to complete a task, and adhering to a schedule. Time management is essential for children's success in school, extracurricular activities, and home life. It helps them balance their responsibilities while still having free time for fun and relaxation. Children who develop good time management skills can reduce their stress and anxiety levels, avoid missing deadlines, and achieve better grades at school. Furthermore, time management promotes independence and responsibility in children, preparing them for work projects in the future. Teaching kids time management skills is crucial, as it is not something that everyone is immediately born with, but rather a skill that is acquired and developed over a long period of time. Parents play a critical role in helping their children develop good time management skills, which can benefit both parents and children throughout their lives. It is vital for children to acquire time management skills, which involve setting goals, planning ahead, monitoring one's own effort and actions, estimating the time necessary to finish an activity, and following step-by-step procedures to complete tasks on time. Let's explore how time management can significantly impact children's lives, reduce stress, improve focus, and enhance their daily organization.

Reduced Stress and Its Benefits

Time management acts as a shield against stress. When children effectively manage their time, they experience fewer moments of rushing and feeling overwhelmed. This reduction in stress is like a breath of fresh air for their young minds.

Imagine your child starting their day calmly, without the frantic rush to catch the school bus or the constant worry of forgetting something essential. With time management in their toolbox, children can approach each day with confidence, knowing they have the skills to handle whatever comes their way.

Improved Focus and Concentration

Another benefit of time management is its ability to supercharge a child's focus and concentration. When they allocate specific time for homework, play, and other activities, they learn to be fully present in the task at hand.

Picture your child sitting down to do their homework with a clear plan in mind. They know they have dedicated time for studying, and there's no need to rush through it. This focused approach allows them to absorb information better, complete their assignments more efficiently, and ultimately excel academically.

Better Organization for Daily Tasks

Lastly, time management is the key to unlocking better organization in a child's daily life. By creating a structured schedule, children learn to prioritize tasks effectively.

Envision your child confidently handling their school assignments, extracurricular activities, and chores without getting overwhelmed. With their time well-organized, they can allocate sufficient time to each task, ensuring that nothing is forgotten or left to the last minute.

REAL-LIFE APPLICATIONS

Let's bring the concept of time management to life with practical examples of how these skills benefit children in various situations.

1. Homework and Study Time

Imagine a child who manages their time wisely, allocating dedicated hours for homework and study. They complete assignments with ease, retain information better, and perform well on tests and exams.

2. Extracurricular Activities

Time management enables children to participate in extracurricular activities without compromising their academics. They strike a balance between school, sports, arts, and other interests, fostering well-rounded development.

3. Chores and Responsibilities

With time management, children efficiently handle chores and responsibilities at home. They learn valuable life skills like cooking, cleaning, organizing, and contributing to a harmonious household.

4. Social Relationships

Time management doesn't mean sacrificing playtime with friends. Instead, it helps children manage their social interactions effectively. They enjoy quality time with friends and family without feeling rushed or stressed.

5. Free Time

Time management creates pockets of free time in a child's day. This free time is essential for relaxation, pursuing hobbies, or simply unwinding, promoting mental and emotional well-being.

HOW TO SPOT IF A CHILD IS STRUGGLING WITH TIME MANAGEMENT

Here are a few characteristics of a child with time management issues:

- Spending too long on one problem or section of an assignment
- Difficulty getting started on tasks
- Struggling to prioritize tasks—for example, working on an assignment due next week (or not working on anything at all) when they have other work that is due the next day
- Consistently working but not finishing assignments or other chores
- Appearing to always be in a rush and being frequently late
- Underestimating how long it will take to complete tasks

Now that we've established why time management is essential for children, let's roll up our sleeves and get to work. In this section, we'll provide practical guidance on developing time management skills, enabling parents and teachers to empower kids with this valuable skill.

STRATEGIES FOR TEACHING TIME MANAGEMENT SKILLS

1. Create a Daily Routine

Kids really thrive on a predictable routine. It provides a feeling of safety. This security frees up their ability to focus on other skills and eventually will lead to building independence. Part of this daily routine should involve teaching our kids how to use a planner or calendar. Make it visual and easy to understand. Break their day into blocks of time for various activities, like school, homework, play, and chores. Ensure they include time for breaks and relaxation. The goal is to give them a plan for their day, helping them understand what comes next. This will help them keep track of their tasks and deadlines while setting goals and prioritizing tasks, which can help children stay focused on their responsibilities. It is essential to start with everyday tasks to practice time estimation, as developing the skill of estimating how long tasks take is necessary for effective time management. Turning time management into a game will really help young kids! My favorite game is Beat the Clock. Set a visual timer and have your child try to finish the task before the timer goes off. This is a great way to help them begin to estimate how long certain activities take to complete. It also demonstrates that time moves on, and they need to get started right away to finish the task.

2. Use Visual Aids

Visual aids are invaluable in teaching time management. They make it easier for children to remember and plan for their responsibilities. Consider making a daily schedule using pictures showing each activity. Post this schedule in an easy-to-see location and refer to it often throughout the day. Post times next to each activity so your child can begin to understand when each activity takes place during the day. Move a colored Post-it Note next to the current activity so your child will know where they are on the schedule. As they get more experience with the schedule, they can be in charge of moving the Post-it Notes throughout the day.

3. Setting and Achieving Goals

Teach your child the art of goal setting. Help them identify short-term and long-term goals. Short-term goals could be completing homework assignments, while long-term goals could involve improving grades in a particular subject. Goals give children a sense of purpose and motivation to manage their time effectively.

4. Break Tasks into Smaller Steps

Large tasks can be daunting, even for adults. For children, breaking tasks into smaller, manageable steps is a game-changer. Guide your child in deconstructing assignments or chores into bite-sized portions. For example, instead of saying, "Clean the bathroom," try being more specific and say, "Wipe down the mirror." This makes the task feel less overwhelming and more achievable.

5. Prioritize Tasks Effectively

Time management isn't just about doing everything; it's about doing the right things at the right time. Teach your child the art of prioritization. Help them understand which tasks are most important and must be tackled first. This skill ensures they focus their time and energy where it matters most.

6. Put Away Distractions

For older children, put smartphones and smartwatches away when trying to complete homework and chores. This will help them focus better on the task at hand.

7. Help Teach Task Initiation for Non-Preferred Activities

This can be the most challenging time management skill for kids and adults to learn. Let's face it! Life is full of desirable distractions —playing games, doing crafts, texting friends, or just daydreaming! Eventually, though, our kids will need to know how to manage their time to get chores and assignments done on time. There are a couple of great ways to teach kids how to complete activities that are not their favorite:

- **Pomodoro Technique:** This strategy is best for older kids, where you set a timer for twenty-five minutes and work that entire time on a chore or assignment. When the timer goes off, take a break for two to three minutes. Continue this pattern until your child finishes the task. For younger kids, set a timer for five minutes and challenge them to work the whole time and then take a break.

- **Eating the Frog Technique:** "Eating the frog" means doing the most challenging task of the day before anything else. If you have two hard tasks, do the most demanding one first. Doing the hardest thing first can make doing the rest of your work seem easier.

8. Teach Ending Times

Help your kids understand how long certain routines should last. For example, explain that getting ready for bed should take ten minutes. Setting an end time creates a sense of urgency so kids know they don't have time to procrastinate.

9. Teach Your Child to Tell Time

After all, how can we expect our kids to manage time if they can't tell time? There is a great app called TimeMachines by Timex, which is designed for early elementary-aged kids. It's a fun way to practice and build time-telling skills.

10. For Smaller Tasks, Have Your Child Pick a Time

If you notice a chore you asked your child to do still isn't done, ask your child to choose a time when they will commit to completing the job. For example, ask: "When will you put your clothes away?" Help your child come up with a time by looking at the daily schedule and pick a time that would work best. Once a time has been decided upon, set a timer to help your child remember when they decided they would do the chore. This helps give kids ownership over their time and their chores.

11. Be Flexible

Teach and model flexibility when it comes to time management. Sometimes, even our best-thought-out plans for getting things done can get derailed by unforeseen obstacles. It's important to teach our kids that perfection is not the goal when it comes to managing our time. We do our best and remember that we can always try again later.

Imagine your child confidently using a schedule, marking dates on a calendar, setting goals, breaking down assignments, and prioritizing tasks. These time management skills lay a strong foundation for success in school and life.

TIPS FOR PARENTS AND TEACHERS

Here are a few extra tips that parents and teachers can use to help children develop these essential skills and create a supportive environment for their growth.

1. Lead by Example

Children learn best through observation. As parents and teachers, demonstrate effective time management in your own lives. Let them see you create schedules, set goals, and prioritize tasks.

2. Open Communication

Encourage open dialogue with children about time management. Ask about their schedules and help them identify areas for improvement. Be patient and empathetic, understanding that they may face challenges along the way.

3. Set Realistic Goals

Guide children in setting achievable goals for themselves. Make sure your goals are clear, easy to measure, and have a deadline. Use these attention milestones to guide you in determining how long you should expect a child to be able to focus on a task:

- 4–6 minutes: 2 years old
- 6–8 minutes: 3 years old
- 8–12 minutes: 4 years old
- 12–18 minutes: 5 years old
- 16–24 minutes: 6 years old
- 24+ minutes: 7 years old
- 1 hour with short 10-minute breaks after 30 minutes: 8 years–adult

Remember, these are just typical milestones, and each person is different. Some kids may be able to focus for longer than these time parameters, and some less. The important thing to remember is to take time for breaks! Celebrate their successes, no matter how small, to boost their confidence.

4. Teach Organization

Show children how to stay organized. Teach them to use tools like calendars, planners, or smartphone apps to keep track of assignments, events, and deadlines.

5. Create a Supportive Environment

- **Designate a Study Space:** Set up a dedicated study area at home where children can focus on their homework and assignments. Ensure it's well-lit and free from distractions.

- **Balanced Schedule:** Strike a balance between school, extracurricular activities, and downtime. Avoid overscheduling, which can lead to stress and burnout.
- **Encourage Independence:** Gradually empower children to take ownership of their schedules. Let them make decisions about allocating time and setting goals, fostering a sense of responsibility.
- **Celebrate Progress:** Recognize and celebrate your child's efforts and improvements in time management. Positive reinforcement goes a long way in motivating them.

To truly appreciate the significance of time management, let's revisit Ben's journey. Ben's transformation began with small but impactful changes. His parents and teachers worked together to help him develop time management skills. They started by helping him create a daily schedule that clearly outlined his responsibilities and activities. Instead of rushing out the door in the morning, Ben first took a few moments to check his schedule to make sure he had everything he needed for the day. The checklist by the front door became his trusted ally, and he made it a habit to review it before leaving. He also set his alarm to go off fifteen minutes earlier, which gave him extra time to get organized in the morning.

The impact of these changes in Ben's morning routine was remarkable. No longer did he race against time, fearing he'd forgotten something crucial. Instead, he left for school with confidence, knowing he had everything in hand. The once stressful mornings transformed into peaceful, organized beginnings to his day. Ben learned to allocate time for tasks such as getting dressed, packing his backpack, and having breakfast, allowing him to leave home without the frantic rush. He was able to do some of these tasks the night before, like packing his backpack and laying out his clothes for the next day. This helped lighten the load of things to do in the morning. As time management became second nature to Ben, he applied these skills to school and other activities. He started using a planner to jot down assignments, tests, and important dates. This simple tool helped him stay on top of his schoolwork. Ben also began setting goals for himself. He aimed to complete his homework before dinner, giving him more time to relax in the evening. Breaking his homework into smaller steps made it easier to manage, and he learned to prioritize assignments based on deadlines. By bedtime, Ben's evenings were no longer chaotic. He finished his homework with focus, thanks to his improved time management skills. This meant he could enjoy quality time with his family and still get to bed on time, ensuring he was well-rested for the next school day.

FUN BOOKS TO READ ABOUT TIME MANAGEMENT

1. *Timmy's Monster Diary: Screen Time Stress* by Raun Melmed and Annette Sexton
2. *Stella Díaz Dreams Big* by Angela Dominguez
3. *Fast Break* by Derek Jeter and Paul Mantell
4. *In a Minute, Mama Bear* by Rachel Bright
5. *I'll Never Get All of That Done!* by Bryan Smith

CONCLUSION

The journey through this chapter has shed light on the vital role of time management in a child's life. Many parents are familiar with the frustration of reminding children to get ready for bed, only to find them still unprepared several minutes later. However, it's crucial to recognize that children facing such challenges are not lazy or disobedient; rather, they may need help developing effective time management skills.

Time management, defined as the art of using time wisely to achieve goals, stay organized, and reduce stress, is a crucial executive functioning skill. As children progress through different stages of learning, the demand for effective time management becomes more evident. The ability to organize information, prioritize tasks, and adhere to schedules is essential for success in school, extracurricular activities, and home life.

This is a significant executive functioning skill because managing your time well helps you feel less stressed, stay focused better, and keep things organized every day. These benefits contribute not only to academic success but also to a child's overall well-being and development.

This chapter explored real-life applications, practical examples, and effective time management strategies for children. From creating daily routines to setting and achieving goals, breaking tasks into smaller steps, and managing distractions, parents and teachers play a vital role in guiding children toward mastering this essential skill.

The transformative journey of Ben, a sixth grader facing time management challenges, serves as an inspiring example. By implementing small but impactful changes, such as creating a daily schedule and using a checklist, Ben experienced positive shifts in his morning routine. These changes extended to various aspects of his life, from academics to extracurricular activities, showcasing the far-reaching benefits of effective time management.

In empowering children with time management skills, parents and teachers contribute to their immediate success and lifelong independence. Through patience, observation, and practical guidance, children can confidently navigate their daily challenges, ultimately laying a solid foundation for success in school and life.

We have explored six important executive function skills so far. Let's take a look now at super skill number seven—working memory.

SUPER SKILL #7: WORKING MEMORY

"Telling a child who struggles with WORKING MEMORY to just focus more, is like telling a person who is hard of hearing to just listen a little harder."

— BECKETT HAIGHT

Have you ever felt like your child wasn't paying attention to you? Ha! Ha! Of course, we have all probably felt this way! Or have you heard from your child's teacher that they struggle to listen and follow directions well? It can be a very frustrating situation, for sure! But let's imagine for a minute that our children were not being defiant in these moments but instead needed help developing their working memory. Instead of getting angry or frustrated when we see our children not paying attention, let's assume good intentions on their part and learn how to become aware of their working memory needs and how we can support them. Working memory is like the brain's notepad; for children, it's a super skill that forms the foundation for successful learning. Imagine a student like Ben from our story trying to navigate his school day without a well-developed working memory. It's like attempting to build a house without a sturdy foundation—the whole structure becomes shaky. In this chapter, we will explore the importance of our seventh super executive functioning skill, working memory. We will examine the concept of working memory, its significance, and how we can help develop this skill in our children.

WORKING MEMORY AT A GLANCE

Working memory is different from some of the other types of memory you might be more familiar with. One of the brain's critical executive functions, it is the ability to work with information without losing track of what we're doing.

To understand this even better, let's take a closer look at the three types of memory that we use:

1. Long-term memory (maintaining understanding)
2. Short-term memory (cramming for a test)
3. Working memory (using new information to complete a task)

Here is a great example to show this concept even better:

Try to remember these numbers, look away, and try to repeat them:

$$4, 6, 2, 5$$

That is short-term memory.

Now, look at the numbers again, look away, and try to add them up. Were you able to do it? It probably wasn't as easy, right? This is an example of working memory.

EXAMPLES OF WHEN WE USE WORKING MEMORY

Working memory is at play in numerous daily situations, even if we may not be consciously aware of it. Here are a few everyday examples:

1. Remembering Directions

When you're given directions to a new place, you use your working memory to hold onto information, such as street names and turns, until you reach your destination.

2. Mental Math

When you calculate a tip at a restaurant or solve a simple math problem in your head, you rely on working memory to store numbers, perform calculations, and arrive at the answer.

3. Following Multi-Step Instructions

Whether it's assembling a piece of furniture or cooking a recipe with several steps, working memory helps you retain the steps and execute them in the correct sequence.

4. Reading Comprehension

When reading a book, your working memory aids in remembering what you've read earlier, making connections between different parts of the text, and comprehending the overall message.

5. Classroom Learning

For students like Ben, working memory is vital for tasks such as listening to the teacher, taking notes, and remembering what was discussed for later recall.

As you can see, working memory plays a pivotal role in our daily lives, particularly in the learning process. It is often described as the "brain's notepad" or the "mental sketchpad." It is the cognitive system responsible for holding and processing information for the short term. Think of working memory as a whiteboard in your mind where you jot down crucial information, manipulate it, and then erase it when it's no longer needed. Working memory keeps new information in your mind for a short time so you can use it and link it with other things you know. But it's not just for the short term—it also helps your brain arrange new information to remember it for a long time. When people struggle with working memory, their brains might store information in a messy way or not store it for long at all. Sometimes, what seems like a problem with working memory is actually an issue with attention, where the brain didn't put the information into its storage system in the first place.

The importance of working memory is well-established, as it has been linked to academic achievement and positive learning outcomes. However, not all children develop working memory at the same rate, and several factors can impact its development. Very young children tend to have a smaller working memory. This is why it is best to give them one-step directions and use very simple language when asking them to complete tasks. As children grow older, their working memory will increase. So, part of the challenge with working memory is simply developmental. However, there are other factors that affect our working memory.

Three of the main circumstances are:

1. When we are distracted
2. When we are trying to hold on to too much information at one time
3. When we are engaged in difficult activities

If you think about it, this describes a large portion of a school day for many kids. And once information is lost from our working memory, we can't get it back because it was never stored in our long-term memory. This solves the mystery surrounding why we as adults have to repeat ourselves to our kids so many times! When information has slipped from their working memory, we need to remember there is no way for them to retrieve this information unless we provide it again. We need to have a lot of patience and understanding to help our kids build this skill!

The brain also implements sustained activation and capacity limits in working memory, with most people only being able to hold on to a few pieces of information in their working memories at one time. Improvements in working memory performance in preschoolers are important, as they have far-reaching conse-quences for children's cognitive development. Factors such as changes in the speed of forgetting, processing speed, and long-term knowledge can contribute to working memory development during early childhood. Children with high working memory capacities have better school achievement than children with low capacities, and deficits in working memory are thought to play a central role in neurodevelopmental disorders such as Attention Deficit Hyperactivity Disorder (ADHD). Poor working memory can significantly affect learning in math, reading comprehension, complex problem-solving, and test-taking. Overall, working memory is crucial to executive functioning and is essential for academic performance.

WHY IS WORKING MEMORY IMPORTANT FOR CHILDREN?

Working memory has been shown to be a better indicator of future academic success than IQ scores, test scores, and even student attitude! Isn't that amazing? A study by Monica Melby-Lervag and Charles Hulme found that children under ten years of age showed significantly greater benefits from verbal working memory training than older children (eleven to eighteen years old) (Melby-Lervåg and Hulme 2013). However, working memory does not work alone; it relies on other executive function skills, such as self-control, attention, and flexible thinking. For this reason, it is so important for parents and teachers to teach these skills to children explicitly and to practice them often. Children with strong working memories have the following characteristics:

1. They can apply previously learned information to new situations.
2. They stay focused and on task.
3. They can reorganize their thoughts to make room for new information.
4. They take better notes and can copy information more accurately.
5. They can follow complex and multi-step directions.

We would all love for our kids to possess these qualities. The good news is that it is possible to help our kids build working memory. It is a skill that can be developed.

FIVE WAYS KIDS EMPLOY WORKING MEMORY TO
ENHANCE CLASSROOM LEARNING

Working memory is like a mental superhero that helps children succeed in various aspects of learning. Understanding how kids use working memory in the classroom can empower parents and teachers to support their development effectively. Here are five ways in which working memory comes into play during the learning process:

1. Information Retention and Recall

Working memory enables children to store and retrieve information as needed. For example, when a teacher provides instructions for a classroom activity, working memory allows children to hold onto those instructions, follow them, and recall them step by step. This skill is fundamental for tasks like solving math problems or completing assignments.

2. Problem-solving and Critical Thinking

When faced with a challenging problem or task, children rely on working memory to break it down into manageable parts. They can hold the problem's details in their minds, consider different strategies, and make decisions based on the information they've stored temporarily. This process is essential for subjects like science and critical thinking activities.

3. Reading Skills

Proficient reading involves working memory in several ways. Children use it to remember the meanings of words encountered in a text, keep track of character relationships and plot developments, and to understand the overall story. Working memory helps them connect the dots between sentences and paragraphs, enhancing comprehension. For younger students, working memory is responsible for many skills used to learn to read, including auditory working memory, which helps kids sound out new words, and visual working memory, which allows them to remember what the words look like so they can recognize them throughout the rest of a sentence.

4. Math Skills

Working memory plays a critical role in mathematical tasks. When solving math problems mentally, children hold numbers in their working memory. For instance, when adding or subtracting, they remember the numbers they're working with and the partial sums or differences as they progress through the calculation.

5. Organization and Time Management

Organizing tasks and managing time effectively requires working memory skills. Children use it to plan their daily routines, remember what assignments are due, and allocate time to different activities, such as, studying, homework, and extracurricular tasks. A strong working memory helps them stay organized and on track.

6. Self-Regulation

As children develop their working memory, they also improve their self-regulation skills. They can better control their impulses, remember instructions, and plan their actions. This is particularly important for tasks like homework, where students must organize their time and complete assignments.

FACTORS IMPACTING THE DEVELOPMENT OF WORKING MEMORY IN CHILDREN

Understanding the factors that can influence the development of working memory in children is useful for parents and teachers. By recognizing these elements, you can provide better support to help children enhance this essential cognitive skill.

1. Age and Maturation

Working memory tends to improve as children grow older. Younger children may have a more limited working memory capacity than older kids. This natural maturation process is one reason why it's essential to tailor expectations and strategies based on a child's age. It is also so important to begin working on memory activities with children during their preschool years.

2. Genetics

Genetics can also play a role in working memory development. Some children may inherit a predisposition for stronger or weaker working memory abilities from their parents. However, genetics is just one piece of the puzzle, and environmental factors also play a significant role.

3. Environment and Stimulation

A stimulating environment that encourages exploration and learning can positively impact working memory development. Exposing children to a variety of experiences, such as reading, puzzles, and educational games, can help exercise and strengthen their working memory.

4. Nutrition and Health

Proper nutrition and overall health are essential for cognitive development, including working memory. Ensure that children receive a balanced diet rich in nutrients that support brain function and promote physical activity to maintain overall health.

5. Sleep

Getting enough sleep is super important for remembering things better and thinking clearly. Lack of sleep can impair working memory and make it challenging for children to focus and learn. Establishing healthy sleep routines is vital.

6. Stress and Emotional Well-Being

Feeling really stressed or anxious can make it hard to remember things. To help kids deal with stress, make sure they're in a caring and comforting environment. Teach them ways to relax, like taking deep breaths or doing mindfulness exercises.

7. Learning Disabilities

Some children may have learning disabilities, such as ADHD or Specific Learning Disabilities (SLD), which can impact working memory. Early identification and appropriate interventions are essential for these children.

8. Classroom Environment

Teachers can create classroom environments that support working memory development. Providing clear instructions, minimizing distractions, and offering opportunities for repetition and practice can be beneficial. Teachers can add visual aids such as posting pictures showing the different steps needed to complete an activity. Numbering these visual aids can further help students keep track of where they are in the process of completing the activity. The most helpful tip is to keep in mind that repeating directions multiple times might be necessary to help kids with working memory weaknesses. Asking students to repeat the directions after you have given them helps them remember the instructions better. It takes a lot of patience!

9. Parental Involvement

Parental involvement in a child's education and cognitive development is crucial. Engage in activities that challenge working memory at home, such as reading together, playing memory games, and discussing daily experiences. These skills are just as important, if not more so, as working on academic skills with your kids at home.

10. Individual Differences

Each child is unique, and working memory development can vary widely from one individual to another. Recognize and celebrate each child's progress and tailor your teaching and support to their specific needs.

HOW TO SPOT WORKING MEMORY CHALLENGES IN CHILDREN

As a parent or teacher, it's essential to be attentive to signs indicating a child is experiencing difficulties with their working memory. Poor working memory is the cause of many concerns parents and teachers have about a child's behavior. Most of the time, we might not even make the connection that working memory is part of the problem. We don't realize that when kids appear to be daydreaming and off task, it's sometimes because their working memory is full! They tune out because their brains literally cannot hold any additional information, and they legitimately cannot follow along. This is why it is helpful to identify these challenges early so we can pave the way for effective support and interventions. Here are some key indicators to look out for:

1. Forgetfulness

If a child frequently forgets tasks or instructions shortly after they've been given, it could be a sign of working memory struggles. For example, they may forget to bring home their homework or fail to follow through with multi-step tasks.

2. Difficulty Following Directions

Children with working memory challenges may struggle to follow verbal or written instructions. They may get lost or confused when asked to complete a series of steps, such as those found in math problems or assignments.

3. Poor Reading Comprehension

Weak working memory can hinder a child's ability to understand and retain what they read. They might have trouble connecting details in a story, remembering character names, or recalling the sequence of events.

4. Inconsistent Performance

If your child's academic performance varies significantly from one day to another, it may be linked to fluctuations in working memory. They may excel on some days when they can focus and remember information but have a hard time on days when their working memory is overloaded.

5. Difficulty with Mental Math

Math can be particularly challenging for children with working memory issues. If your child has difficulty performing calculations mentally, struggles with remembering numbers during math problems, or frequently makes calculation errors, these could be signs of working memory challenges.

6. Impulsivity and Disorganization

Weak working memory can lead to impulsive behavior and disorganization. Your child may act without thinking through the consequences or have trouble planning and managing their time effectively.

7. Emotional Struggles

Working memory challenges can be frustrating for children. If you notice signs of frustration, anxiety, or a lack of confidence related to schoolwork or tasks requiring memory, this could be an indication of working memory difficulties.

8. Frequently Distracted

Children with working memory issues may be easily distracted because they struggle to hold on to information or instructions in their minds. They may also have difficulty maintaining focus in class or while doing homework.

9. Slow Processing Speed

Slower than expected processing speed can also be linked to working memory challenges. Your child may take more time than their peers to complete tasks that involve memory, such as reading, writing, or problem-solving.

10. Teacher and Caregiver Feedback

Pay attention to feedback from teachers and other caregivers. They may observe signs of working memory challenges in the classroom or during daily activities. Regular communication with educators is valuable in identifying and addressing these issues.

If you notice these signs in your child, it's important not to jump to conclusions but to seek professional guidance. A comprehensive evaluation by an educational psychologist or specialist can provide a clearer picture of your child's working memory strengths and challenges. Children can improve their working memory skills and excel academically with proper support and strategies.

STRATEGIES TO DEVELOP WORKING MEMORY IN CHILDREN

Research has shown that challenging children with new skills can benefit working memory development. Slowly increasing demands on working memory can also aid in its development. Overall, developing strong working memory skills is crucial for maintaining focus and concentration in children and significantly impacts academic achievement and learning outcomes. Here are several ways we can help build this skill:

1. Engage in Memory Games

Simple memory games like the electronic Hasbro Simon memory game or card matching games like Memory can be fun ways to exercise working memory. They encourage children to remember sequences of actions or matching pairs of cards. Here are a few other examples of fun memory games:

- **Distraction:** This game can be played as a family or in the classroom. You can buy the game on Amazon! Players take turns picking number cards and have to remember the order of the numbers they pick. But if someone gets a distraction card, they must answer a funny question before saying the numbers in the correct order.
- **Scrabble:** This is a great game for working memory and also helps support planning and organization skills! Kids need to plan and think ahead about how to make their own words using the ones other players have already used.
- **Shopping List:** This is another game available on Amazon. It is a twist on the classic concentration game. Players try to find all of the items on their shopping list. As other

players turn your items over, you need to remember where your items are so you can find them on your turn.

- **Remember 10 with Ben:** This is a fun working memory activity book that helps kids learn how to remember things through various games. Each part of the book has ten things Ben must remember and a tip to help your child remember the items for Ben. This is also available on Amazon.
- **Card Games:** Go Fish, Blink, and Uno Moo are excellent games to try.

2. Practice Mindfulness

Mindfulness exercises that promote focus and attention can indirectly benefit working memory. Breathing exercises and guided imagery can help children become more aware of their thoughts and enhance their mental control. Here are a couple of ideas to try:

Pennies Game: This game is good for kids aged three and up and can be played alone or with friends. All you need is a penny for each player and a basket.

Here's how to play:

1. Give each player a penny and give them one minute to look at it closely, paying attention to all the details.
2. Put all the pennies in the basket.
3. Let each player try to find their penny in the basket.
4. When players take their penny, they should explain how they knew it was theirs.
5. You can also play this game with other objects. The important thing is that the kids can focus and pay attention to details.

Breathe with a Pinwheel: First, get two pinwheels—one for you and one for your child. Then, do these five things:

1. Sit up straight with a relaxed body.
2. Breathe deeply on your pinwheels together. How do you both feel? Are you calm or having trouble sitting still?
3. Now, blow on your pinwheels quickly. How do you feel now? Is it different from when you breathe deeply?
4. Breathe on the pinwheels normally. Pay attention to how you feel.
5. Talk about the different ways you breathed and how they made you feel.

3. Chunk Information

Help children break down information into smaller chunks. For instance, when learning a new phone number, divide it into segments, making it easier to remember.

4. Provide Visual Aids

Visual aids, such as charts, diagrams, and mind maps, can assist children in organizing information spatially, reducing the load on their working memory. Teachers can help support working memory by writing instructions on the board or posting numbered pictures showing the steps needed to complete an activity. Many resources can be found on the website Teachers Pay Teachers by searching "visual directions" in the search bar.

5. Encourage Active Reading

While reading, ask children to pause and summarize what they've read or predict what might happen next. This not only boosts comprehension but also engages their working memory.

6. Try Using Audiobooks to Build Comprehension Skills

An audiobook changes the input method the child is receiving. If your child struggles to sound out words, this method removes the difficult task of decoding words from the picture, which lightens the child's cognitive load and allows them to focus on meaning.

7. Support a Healthy Lifestyle

Ensure children get enough sleep, engage in physical activity, and maintain a balanced diet. These factors can impact cognitive functions, including working memory.

8. Offer Consistent Routines

Establishing routines can reduce cognitive load by making daily activities predictable. When children know what to expect, they can focus more on the task at hand.

9. Multisensory Learning

Encourage children to engage multiple senses when learning new information. For example, when studying vocabulary, they can write the word, say it aloud, and create a visual image to enhance memory retention.

10. Use Mnemonics

Mnemonics, such as acronyms or rhymes, can be helpful memory aids. Encourage children to create their own mnemonics for challenging concepts or lists. For example, to remember the names and order of the planets, you can use this mnemonic: **My V**ery **E**arthly **M**other **J**ust **S**erved **U**s **N**ine **P**izzas. In this example, the first letter of each word represents the planet names. (Mercury, Venus, Earth, Mars, Jupiter, Saturn, Uranus, Neptune, and Pluto—now considered a dwarf planet) This is how I remembered the names and order of the planets when Pluto was still considered a planet!

11. Break Tasks into Steps

When faced with complex tasks or projects, guide children in breaking them down into smaller, sequential steps. This approach makes remembering and executing each part of the task easier.

12. Encourage Self-Reflection

Teach children to reflect on their thought processes and strategies when solving problems or completing tasks. This self-awareness can help them identify which techniques work best for them and refine their working memory skills accordingly.

13. Provide Positive Reinforcement

Praise and positive reinforcement can motivate children to practice working memory strategies consistently. Acknowledge their efforts and progress, fostering a growth mindset.

14. Seek Professional Help

If your child's working memory challenges significantly affect their academic performance, consider consulting with an educational psychologist or specialist. They can provide tailored interventions and strategies.

BEN'S JOURNEY: STRENGTHENING WORKING MEMORY

Let's revisit Ben, the sixth grader we met earlier. Ben had been facing several challenges related to working memory. He often forgot important items and struggled to follow through on instructions. His working memory issues made school a daily hurdle, impacting his academic performance and social interactions. Let's look at how the strategies in this chapter helped Ben.

Ben's journey took a positive turn when his parents and teachers began implementing strategies to strengthen his working memory. Here's how these practical techniques made a significant difference in Ben's life:

1. Memory Games and Activities

Ben started playing memory-boosting games like Chess and Uno with his family and friends. These games not only improved his memory but also made learning fun. He even began to choose these activities over his video games occasionally.

2. Visual Aids

With the help of visual aids, like charts, diagrams, and task plans, Ben learned to organize his work visually. He learned to create a task plan by writing down the steps needed to complete an assignment, using different-colored pens for each step. Ben realized that using numbers, rather than bullet points, to label directions helped him keep track of where he was in the process of completing an assignment. He discovered sticky notes were helpful to use for this purpose. This way, each time he completed a step, he could peel away the sticky note and move on to the next step. He also learned how to use mind maps to break down complex subjects into more manageable parts, reducing the cognitive load on his working memory.

3. Chunking Information

Ben practiced breaking down information into smaller chunks, which made it easier for him to remember and process. For instance, he started grouping his daily tasks, ensuring he didn't forget any essential items before leaving for school.

4. Active Reading

Ben's reading comprehension improved significantly as he started actively reading. He learned to pause while reading, summarize what he had read, jot down notes, and predict what would happen next in the story. These strategies enhanced his understanding of the material. When he was feeling overwhelmed, Ben would listen to audiobooks for a change of pace. This made reading less stressful.

5. Mindful Breathing and Focus

Ben's parents introduced him to mindfulness exercises, including deep breathing techniques. These exercises helped calm his mind and increase his attention span, indirectly supporting his working memory.

6. Establishing Routines

Ben reduced the mental effort required to plan his day by establishing consistent daily routines. He knew exactly what to expect in the morning, during homework time, and at bedtime, allowing his working memory to focus on other tasks.

7. Multisensory Learning

Ben started engaging multiple senses when learning new information. For example, when studying vocabulary, he would write the words, say them aloud, and draw pictures to go with the words. This multisensory approach made learning more engaging and memorable.

Ben's journey is an inspiring example of how practical working memory strategies can transform a child's educational experience. As parents and teachers, we can draw valuable lessons from his story and apply the same techniques to support our kids or students.

Remember that each child is unique, and the strategies may need to be tailored to individual needs and preferences. Regular communication with children, observing their progress, and providing positive reinforcement are essential aspects of helping them strengthen their working memory skills.

CONCLUSION

In this chapter, we learned that working memory is a crucial executive functioning skill that forms the foundation for successful learning in children. Working memory is important in various aspects of academic success, including reading, mathematics, problem-solving, and self-regulation. We learned that working memory is not only a short-term tool but also contributes to organizing information for long-term storage. Working memory is like a mental muscle that can be strengthened with practice and support. Each child's uniqueness and the need for tailored strategies are necessary considerations when working with children facing challenges. Ongoing communication between parents and teachers, observation, and positive reinforcement are greatly needed in the journey of helping children strengthen their working memory skills.

If we can spot when kids are having trouble with their memory early on, we can help them out a lot. There are several ways we can do this!

One big thing is to notice when kids are having a hard time remembering things, like instructions or tasks. Then, we can use fun games and activities to give their memory a workout. Simple games like matching cards can be super helpful and make learning fun.

We can also teach kids how to stay calm and focused, which indirectly helps their memory. Breathing exercises are one way to do this. Plus, breaking down big tasks into smaller steps can make it easier for kids to remember what to do. Using pictures and diagrams can also be a big help. They show information in a way that's easier for kids to understand and remember. And when teachers give clear instructions and make sure there aren't too many distractions in the classroom, it's easier for kids to focus and remember things. Reading together, sticking to a routine, and doing activities that use all the senses (like drawing while saying things out loud) are other ways we can help kids boost their memory skills. And don't forget to cheer them on and tell them when they're doing a great job! Positive feedback can make a big difference.

Parents and teachers play a vital role in nurturing this super skill in children, setting them up for success in school and beyond.

GETTING HELP AND SUPPORT
FOR CHILDREN

"Beneath every behavior there is a feeling, and beneath each feeling is a need, and when we meet the need, rather than focus on the behavior, we begin to deal with the cause, not the symptom"

— *ASHLEIGH WARNER*

It can be extremely challenging for parents, caregivers, and teachers to know how to get the help and support they need to best assist the children in their care. I have seen many children struggle in my classroom over the years and, at times, have felt helpless trying to get them the support they needed to have more successful days at school. So, I know first-hand that the struggle is real. It is also impossible to expect that, as teachers or parents, we will automatically know how to intervene and help a child who is struggling with executive functioning skills. If you suspect a child is struggling with executive functioning or needs extra support at home and school, do not hesitate to reach out for help from a professional. A great place to start is by reaching out to your child's pediatrician. Parents can ask their pediatrician to give them a behavioral inventory for teachers to fill out. This will help your doctor better understand what is happening in the classroom and suggest the next step. Other great resources are school counselors and executive functioning coaches. Schools can also provide accommodations for students facing learning challenges. When children have difficulties with their schoolwork or behavior, schools have a procedure to identify the root of these challenges. It's known as a "special education evaluation," aimed at determining whether a child has a disability and requires tailored teaching and assistance.

The evaluation process includes several steps:

- Agreement between the school and family that the child needs an evaluation.
- Gathering school-related information such as test results and disciplinary records.
- Distributing questionnaires to teachers, parents, or caregivers, sometimes even to the child, to gain a comprehensive understanding of the child's performance at school and home.
- Psychological testing is conducted to assess the child's cognitive abilities and problem-solving skills.
- Additional assessments by other professionals, like speech therapists, especially for children struggling with communication.
- Observation of the child's behavior in a classroom or school environment.
- A meeting will be held to review the evaluation's results and determine if the child qualifies for special education support.

Federal law requires schools to complete the evaluation process within sixty days, although some states may have shorter deadlines.

The evaluation process can evoke various emotions in families. However, after completion, they should have a clearer understanding of their child's strengths and weaknesses and how best to support their development. This is more important than anything! While it can be hard to think about our kids having learning differences from their peers, it is far more heartbreaking to watch kids try to meet the expectations of their parents and teachers and not be able to because they need a different approach to help them learn. When a kid's needs are not met, we will often start seeing behavioral problems. This challenging behavior leads to getting into trouble, which leads to kids not feeling good about themselves. You can see how this can spiral out of control for a child. The truth is no one learns the same way! And finding out how your child learns is the best gift you can give them: the gift to learn and grow according to their unique brain, a chance to be the best they can be. With this gift comes self-confidence, self-awareness, and a joy for learning. To learn more, explore the advantages of undergoing an evaluation, and the different types available, such as free school evaluations versus private ones and assessments specifically for executive dysfunction.

Building a Strong Foundation

Whether we're teachers or parents, we all want our children to do well. Executive functioning skills are the key; they're the foundation on which we can build everything else. Take a moment now to share this book with more readers and get this message out.

Simply by sharing your honest opinion of this book and a little about what you've learned here, you'll help connect this information with the people who are looking for it.

Thank you for your support. It takes a community to raise a child, and we are all part of that community.

Scan the QR code below

CONCLUSION

"Executive Functioning is the foundation for all learning!"

— *TERA SUMPTER*

This book has explored the vital world of executive function skills in children, shedding light on their significance in various aspects of their lives. We've journeyed through seven super skills,

their importance, strategies for development, and real-world applications. These skills are not

just tools for success; they are essential building blocks for a fulfilling and productive life.

I remember beginning my student teaching! I was so excited to get into the classroom and teach amazing lessons. I spent hours planning and prepping all the materials I needed to teach an engaging lesson. I had puppets, hands-on materials, and fun science experiments all planned out to wow my first-grade class. And then reality hit! I stood in front of my class, ready to teach all about the rainforest. I couldn't get more than a few sentences out before students started interrupting me. When we finally made it through the lesson and began to work on some projects I had introduced, mass chaos ensued. I had several kids rushing up to me, saying they couldn't remember what to do. The learning centers I had so painstakingly organized were being destroyed by students who struggled to share the materials. I realized quickly that it didn't matter how fabulous my lessons were; if I couldn't figure out how to manage student behaviors, no one would be learning much of anything!

So, I decided to do what any well-meaning student teacher would do in this case. I went to the bookstore and bought almost every book I could find on classroom management. It was 1994, after all, and the internet wasn't really a thing yet! I followed the directions exactly as they were laid out in the books. I arranged my students into cooperative learning groups. I gave points to the groups that began working quietly on their assignments. I handed out prizes to the groups that earned the most points. Oh boy! That was a huge mistake! Now, I had kids crying because they didn't get a prize. It was not at all what I had imagined teaching would be! I pictured a classroom full of happy, engaged children eager to learn anything I presented to them. Looking back on it all now, I'm not sure how I survived student teaching.

Fast forward to a year later, I was able to get a teaching position working at a beautiful independent school. Again, I was so excited to begin my teaching career. Things went much better this time around. I had learned a few classroom management skills that worked well. However, I was still experiencing behavior problems with several students: students who needed help to listen during lessons, share materials with their classmates, follow simple directions, work independently, and keep their hands and feet to themselves. These were just a few of the troublesome behaviors I noticed in the classroom.

The school I work at is considered a college preparatory school. Even our early childhood programs are advertised as academic, not play-based. Our parents are heavily involved in their children's education. There is a huge emphasis placed on academic learning, especially reading. Many families expect their children to be reading by the end of preschool, and if they aren't, they are very concerned.

As a result, I began to see children exhibit stress as their play time decreased and their academic activities increased. As technology became more prevalent in homes and the classroom, I noticed kids' attention spans were shrinking. It became nearly impossible to hold a child's attention without using an interactive whiteboard. My students struggled to sit and listen to stories, and it was even more challenging for them to listen during lessons. I wanted to figure out why my students were having such a hard time with self-control, attention, and task initiation. I wondered why they couldn't seem to remember my directions even after I had just told them. Then, one day, I ordered a book by Tera Sumpter called *Seeds of Learning*. It was a book about executive function and how necessary these skills are to help children get the most out of their learning. It changed my outlook on education.

As an early childhood educator of twenty-six years, I have had a lot of experience working with young kids. I've learned how to teach young children reading, math, writing, handwriting, social skills, and so much more. However, a big missing piece for me, and I am sure for several other educators, was that I really did not know much about executive functioning or how to develop these skills in my students.

I first heard of executive functioning skills during an educational conference I attended several years ago. I thought it was very interesting, and I saw students in my class who struggled with these skills. This is when it really hit me. We need to TEACH our kids these executive functioning skills just as we teach academic skills. Sure, some kids naturally have better self-control than others. Still, when we notice students struggling with these skills, it gives us an opportunity to step in and explicitly teach them. This is precisely what Tera Sumpter means when she says: "first, executive function, then learning" (Sumpter 2024b). Kids can't learn when they are hungry, tired, stressed, or upset. The same is true for some students who need support with their executive functioning skills.

As parents, educators, and caregivers, we are responsible for nurturing and cultivating these skills in our children. They are not mere attributes but the keys to unlocking a child's full potential. By imparting these skills, we empower children to become independent learners and flexible thinkers, helping them navigate life's challenges with confidence and resilience.

Let us recall that executive function challenges are often misunderstood and misinterpreted. According to Judy Willis, a neurologist and classroom teacher, "We would never think to get mad at a child for not knowing how to read, spell, write or know their math facts. Instead, we would find ways to teach and guide them to a path of success. Therefore, when we see a child melting down, acting impulsively, losing materials, procrastinating, or daydreaming, we need to shift our thinking and consider that these are skills that a child needs to learn. Just like learning the sounds of the alphabet, we need to learn how to be organized, resist lashing out, or plan ahead. If we change our mindset and recognize that teaching our children these critical skills is just as important as teaching reading, math, and writing, there will be more learning taking place rather than frustration, sadness, and avoidance. These skills not only help with academics but also with family and social life" (McIver and Willis, 2022). Instead of labeling children, let us equip them with the strategies and tools they need to flourish. If we do this, we can work on correcting many common behavioral issues at the source. This might mean parents and educators need to adjust their focus from just teaching ABCs and 123s to also teaching executive function skills. By addressing the core executive function processes, we pave the way for lifelong benefits and opportunities for our children.

Remember our student Ben from earlier chapters? His story serves as a beacon of hope and inspiration. His struggles with executive functioning skills mirror those of countless children. Yet, through dedicated efforts and applying these super skills, Ben transformed his life. He overcame obstacles, learned to manage his time effectively, and sharpened his working memory, ultimately achieving success in his academic journey.

I hope this book will help parents and educators take action to create change for our children. Let us invest in developing these super skills, knowing that we are shaping our children's future. Together, we can empower the next generation to reach new heights, to dream big, and to embrace the limitless possibilities that await them.

WORKS CITED

American Academy of Pediatrics. 2021. Beyond Screen Time: A Parent's Guide to Media Use. *Patient Education Online* (1. January).

Anon. 2019. How to help kids develop a growth mindset and build resilience and grit. *Playful Notes*. August. https://playfulnotes.com (accessed: 21. April 2024).

Anon. 2022. Home. *Playful Notes*. 23. November. https://playfulnotes.com/.

Anon. Screen time limits for young children. https://www.aap.org/en/patient-care/media-and-children/center-of-excellence-on-social-media-and-youth-mental-health/qa-portal/qa-portal-library/qa-portal-library-questions/screen-time-limits-for-young-children/.

Center on the Developing Child. 2012. Executive Function & Self-Regulation. *www.developingchild.harvard.edu.* https://developingchild.harvard.edu/science/key-concepts/executive-function/ (accessed: 28. April 2024).

Child Mind Institute and Matthew Rouse. 2024. Child Mind Institute | Transforming Children's Lives/: How can we help kids Self-Regulate? *Child Mind Institute.* 2. April. https://childmind.org/ (accessed: 23. April 2024).

Cohen, Siggie [Dr. Siggie]. 2024. Boundaries are not questions. *Instagram.* 25. January. https://www.instagram.com/dr.siggie (accessed: 23. April 2024).

Conscious Discipline. 2020. Resource: Safe Place Breathing Icons - Conscious Discipline. *Conscious Discipline.* 28. April. https://consciousdiscipline.com

Dyslexia Inspired. 2023. "Every social, learning, work, and living interaction requires executive function skills." *Facebook.* https://www.facebook.com/DyslexiaInspired/ (accessed: 28. April 2024).

Elmore, Tim. 2014. *12 Huge Mistakes Parents Can Avoid: Leading your kids to Succeed in life.* Harvest House.

Griffin, Mark. 2024. What is Self-Control? *Understood.org.* https://www.understood.org (accessed: 23. April 2024).

MacDonald, Kaitlyn. 2019. Five Ways You Can Cultivate Agency in Your Child. *Sparhawk School.* 31. October. https://www.sparhawkschool.com/about-us/blog/post/~board/blog/post/five-ways-you-can-cultivate-agency-in-your-child (accessed: 24. April 2024).

Mattke, Angela. Screen Time and Children: How to guide your child. *Mayo Clinic.* https://www.mayoclinic.org (accessed: 23. April 2024).

McCoy, Jazmine. 2020. Home The Mom Psychologist. *The Mom Psychologist.* https://themompsychologist.com/ (accessed: 23. April 2024).

McIver, Marcy, and Judy Willis. 2022. What are Executive Functioning Skills, and how are they Important in Learning to Read? *Orton Gillingham Online Tutor.* https://www.ortongillinghamonlinetutor.com (accessed: 28. April 2024).

Melby-Lervåg, Monica and Charles Hulme. 2013. Is working memory training effective? A meta-analytic review. *Developmental Psychology* 49, Nr. 2 (1. January): 270–291.

Sumpter, Tera. 2023a. Executive Function is the foundation for learning. *Instagram.* 9. January. https://www.instagram.com/p/C14TVhXOpgF/ (accessed: 28. April 2024).

---. 2023b. Inhibition is the ability to restrain ourselves from doing something now in order to reach a particular goal later in the future. *Instagram.* 10. April. https://www.instagram.com/p/Cq27mmTOBOk (accessed: 24. April 2024).

---. 2023c. The development of self-direction requires agency. If you don't allow children, even very young children, agency, they will struggle to develop self-direction. *Instagram.* 18. April. https://www.instagram.com/p/CrMFAkmvMR7 (accessed: 24. April 2024).

---. 2023d. Helping Children Develop Effective Self-Monitoring and Self-Regulation — Tera Sumpter. *Tera Sumpter.* 23. November. https://terasumpter.com/blog/helping-children-develop-effective-self-monitoring-and-self-regulation.

---. 2024a. Executive functioning is the foundation for learning. *Instagram.* 9. January. https://www.instagram.com/p/C14TVhXOpgF (accessed: 24. April 2024).

---. 2024b. first executive function, then learning. *Instagram.* 5. April. https://www.instagram.com/p/C5Yz11Sx3tU/ (accessed: 1. May 2024).

---. 2024c. Inhibition is an executive function skill of restraint, and it involves three processes. *Instagram.* 11. April. https://www.instagram.com/terasumpter_slp/p/C5nq0RTOlDM (accessed: 1. May 2024).

Sumpter, Tera [@terasumpter_slp]. 2023. "Executive Functioning is the foundation for all learning!" *Instagram.* May. https://instagram.com/@terasumpter_slp (accessed: 21. April 2024).

Tarullo, Amanda. 2022a. When children enter kindergarten, the key question is not whether they know the alphabet or can add and subtract. Instead, the important skills include impulse control, attention span, and emotional regulation. *Instagram.* 4. August. https://www.instagram.com/p/Cg1k157uiqC/.

---. 2022b. "These abilities don't develop on their own. Instead, the relevant regions of the brain need to be activated — and often, since the brain's networks are strengthened through practice.". *Instagram.* 4. August. https://www.instagram.com/p/Cg1k157uiqC/ (accessed: 3. May 2024).

Vanderwier, Jess [Nurtured First]. 2024. "Imagine in your mind there is a big table with lots of chairs. At one seat, there is someone named Worry. In the other chairs are Anger, Excitement, Jealousy, and Sadness... And, at the head of the table, there is someone tall and strong - it's you!" *Nurtured First.* 18. January. https://nurturedfirst.com/ (accessed: 19. April 2024).

VanDeVelde, Christine. 2007. Carol Dweck: Praising Intelligence: Costs to Children's Self-Esteem and Motivation. *The Bing Times* 2007 (1. November). https://bingschool.stanford.edu/news/carol-dweck-praising-intelligence-costs-childrens-self-esteem-and-motivation.

Xplor. 2022. Agency in early childhood—a child's right to choose. *Xplor Education.* 18. February. https://www.ourxplor.com (accessed: 24. April 2024).

REFERENCES

Additude. 'Working Memory Deficit: Symptom Test for Children', 6 June 2022. https://www.additudemag.com/working-memory-deficit-weak-short-term-memory-symptoms-test-children/.

Amely, A. 'Books That Teach Self-Control.' Heart and Mind Teaching, 20 January 2024. https://heartandmindteaching.com/.

Asana. 'The Eisenhower Matrix: How to Prioritize Your To-Do List [2024]'. Asana, 4 October 2022. https://asana.com/resources/eisenhower-matrix.

Australian Education Research Organisation. 'Executive Function and Self-Regulation', 14 September 2021. https://www.edresearch.edu.au/guides-resources/practice-guides/executive-function-and-self-regulation-practice-guide-full-publication.

Basso, Cindy. 'Flexible Thinking'. Socially Skilled Kids, n.d. https://www.sociallyskilledkids.com/flexible-thinking.

Beck, Coleen. 'Games to Help Kids Improve Executive Function.' The OT Toolbox, 27 November 2023. https://www.theottoolbox.com/.

Beck, Colleen. 'Executive Functioning Skills- Teach Planning and Prioritization'. *The OT Toolbox* (blog), 15 February 2019. https://www.theottoolbox.com/executive-functioning-skills-planning-prioritization/.

Belsky, Gail. 'Trouble with Flexible Thinking: Why Some Kids Only See Things One Way.' Understood, 22 November 2023. https://www.understood.org/en/articles/flexible-thinking-what-you-need-to-know.

———. 'What Is Executive Function?' Understood, 27 November 2023. https://www.understood.org/en/articles/what-is-executive-function.

Bethel, Stephannie. 'Cognitive Flexibility | Executive Functions'. Stephanie Bethany | Autistic Adult, 15 June 2021. https://www.stephaniebethany.com/blog/cognitive-flexibility-executive-functions.

Brown, Amber, and Corey Lof. 'Parent Guide for Therapeutic Play'. *Occupational Therapy Capstones*, 1 January 2016. https://commons.und.edu/ot-grad/32.

Bull, Rebecca, Kimberly Andrews Espy, and Sandra A. Wiebe. 'Short-Term Memory, Working Memory, and Executive Functioning in Preschoolers: Longitudinal Predictors of Mathematical Achievement at Age 7 Years'. *Developmental Neuropsychology* 33, no. 3 (2008): 205–28. https://doi.org/10.1080/87565640801982312.

Center on the Developing Child at Harvard University. 'Executive Function &

Self-Regulation', 2 March 2020. https://developingchild.harvard.edu/science/key-concepts/executive-function/.

Cherry, Kendra. 'How to Improve Your Self-Control'. Verywell Mind, n.d. https://www.verywellmind.com/psychology-of-self-control-4177125.

Child Mind Institute. 2024. Helping Kids with Flexible Thinking. *Childmind.org*. 8. March. https://www.childmind.org (accessed: 4. May 2024).

Cohen, Siggie. 'Boundaries Are Not Questions.' Instagram, 25 January 2024. https://www.instagram.com/dr.siggie/.

Connolly, M. 'Self-Regulation Strategies for Kids with Sensory Processing Disorder'. buildlearnthrive, 19 November 2019. https://www.buildlearnthrive.com/post/self-regulation-strategies-for-kids-with-sensory-processing-disorder.

Dajani, Dina R., and Lucina Q. Uddin. 'Demystifying Cognitive Flexibility: Implications for Clinical and Developmental Neuroscience.' *Trends in Neurosciences* 38, no. 9 (September 2015): 571–78. https://doi.org/10.1016/j.tins.2015.07.003.

Dewar, Gwen. 'Teaching Self-Control: Evidence-Based Tips.' PARENTING SCIENCE, 18 November 2023. https://parentingscience.com/teaching-self-control/.

Dourish, Julia. 'Self-Regulation and Executive Function'. Twinkl, 2021. https://www.twinkl.com.ph/blog/key-feature-6-self-regulation-and-executive-function.

Fitzgerald, Meghan. 'Helping Kids Develop Cognitive Flexibility'. Tinkergarten, n.d. https://tinkergarten.com/blog/6-ways-to-help-your-kids-develop-cognitive-flexibility.

Garska Rodriguez, Stacey. '10 Tips for Teaching Kids Time Management'. *The Soccer Mom Blog* (blog), 29 January 2020. https://thesoccermomblog.com/teaching-kids-time-management/.

Ger, Ebru, and Claudia M. Roebers. 'The Relationship between Executive Functions, Working Memory, and Intelligence in Kindergarten Children.' *Journal of Intelligence* 11, no. 4 (April 2023): 64. https://doi.org/10.3390/jintelligence11040064.

Griffin, Kim. 'Sensory Regulation Strategies - How You Can Use Them to Help Your Child.' *GriffinOT* (blog), 11 May 2020. https://www.griffinot.com/sensory-regulation-strategies-what-are-they-and-how-can-they-help-your-child/.

Griffin, Mark. 'What Is Self-Control?' Understood, 5 October 2023. https://www.understood.org/en/articles/self-control-what-it-means-for-kids.

Grogan, Alisha. 'Sensory Self Regulation: A Critical Skill for Kids with Sensory

"Issues." Your Kid's Table, 29 March 2022. https://yourkidstable.com/sensory-self-regulation/.

Holder, Christen. 'Organized and On Time: Tips for Executive Functioning for Kids.' Le Bonheur Children's Hospital, n.d. https://www.lebonheur.org/blogs/practical-parenting/organized-and-on-time-tips-for-executive-functioning-for-kids.

Hunter, Amanda. 'Sensory Processing and Self-Regulation.' Catcote Academy, 2019. https://www.catcoteacademy.co.uk/wp-content/uploads/2020/07/sensory-processing-booklet-for-parents.pdf.

ICT. 'Executive Function Skills & Language'. INTEGRATED CHILDREN'S THERAPY, 24 July 2018. https://integratedchildrens.com/executive-function-skills-language/.

——. 'Executive Function Skills Part 1: What Is Working Memory?' INTEGRATED CHILDREN'S THERAPY, 28 January 2021. https://integratedchildrens.com/executive-function-skills-part-1-what-is-working-memory/.

Jacobson, Rae. 'Helping Kids With Flexible Thinking'. Child Mind Institute, 19 February 2024. https://childmind.org/article/helping-kids-with-flexible-thinking/.

Jacobson, Rae, Matthew Cruger, and Linda Hecker. 'How to Help Kids With Working Memory Issues.' Child Mind Institute, 30 October 2023. https://childmind.org/article/how-to-help-kids-with-working-memory-issues/.

Keiki Early Learning. 'Supporting Children's Sense of Agency', 6 May 2019. https://keikiearlylearning.com.au/supporting-childrens-sense-of-agency/.

Kessler, Colleen. '7 Executive Functioning Activities for Small Children'. Raising Lifelong Learners, 16 July 2021. https://raisinglifelonglearners.com/executive-functioning-activities-for-small-children/.

Kid Sense Child Development. 'Working Memory', 5 January 2023. https://childdevelopment.com.au/areas-of-concern/working-memory/.

Klein, Karen. 'Why Should We Teach Our Kids FLEXIBLE THINKING?' *Karen Klein Blog* (blog), 20 November 2021. https://blog.karenkleinglobal.com/why-and-how-to-teach-our-kids-flexible-thinking/.

Lancia, Gabriella. '12 Self-Control Activities for Kids (Incl. Worksheets)'. Positive-Psychology.com, 1 July 2021. https://positivepsychology.com/self-control-for-kids/.

Litman, Jessica. '12 Best Kids' Books On Organizing And Tidying'. The Organized Mama, 13 November 2019. https://www.theorganizedmama.com/12-best-kids-books-on-organizing-and-tidying/.

MacDonald, K. 'Five Ways You Can Cultivate Agency in Your Child.' Child Mind Institute, 8 October 2019. https://childmind.org/.

Makowski, Mary, and Christine MacDonald. 'What Is Cognitive Flexibility and

How Do I Help My Child With It?' Foothills Academy, 1 December 2020. https://www.foothillsacademy.org/community/articles/cognitive-flexibility.

Martin. '48 Positive Affirmations for Kids'. *Cosmic Kids* (blog), 30 January 2023. https://cosmickids.com/positive-affirmations-for-kids/.

Morin, Amanda. '4 Ways Kids Use Organization Skills to Learn'. Understood, 22 November 2023. https://www.understood.org/en/articles/4-ways-kids-use-organization-skills-to-learn.

——. '5 Ways Kids Use Working Memory to Learn'. Understood, 22 November 2023. https://www.understood.org/en/articles/5-ways-kids-use-working-memory-to-learn.

——. '6 Steps for Breaking down Assignments'. Understood, 5 October 2023. https://www.understood.org/en/articles/6-simple-steps-for-breaking-down-assignments.

——. '8 Working Memory Boosters'. Understood, 28 November 2023. https://www.understood.org/en/articles/8-working-memory-boosters.

——. 'Classroom Accommodations for Executive Function Challenges.' Understood, 5 October 2023. https://www.understood.org/en/articles/classroom-accommodations-executive-function-challenges.

——. 'Self-Care for Kids: 6 Ways to Self-Regulate'. Understood, 27 November 2023. https://www.understood.org/en/articles/self-care-for-kids-6-ways-to-self-regulate.

——. 'Understanding Behavior as Communication: A Teacher's Guide'. Understood, 5 October 2023. https://www.understood.org/en/articles/understanding-behavior-as-communication-a-teachers-guide.

Muriel, Clara. 'Impulse Control Activities for Kids: Fun Games, Activities & Resources to Practice Self-Control at Home or School.' *Very Special Tales* (blog), 17 September 2020. https://veryspecialtales.com/impulse-control-activities-kids/.

O'Donnell, Lauren M. (Ed.). 'Teaching Your Child Self-Control (for Parents).' Nemours Kids Health, June 2018. https://kidshealth.org/en/parents/self-control.html.

Pierce, Rebekah. '16 Tips For Teaching The Art Of Prioritization'. Life Skills Advocate, 29 July 2023. https://lifeskillsadvocate.com/blog/16-tips-for-teaching-the-art-of-prioritization/.

Planning- Cognitive Skill. 'CogniFit', 10 August 2016. https://www.cognifit.com/science/planning.

Playful Notes. 'The Best Growth Mindset Activities That Will Encourage Kids to Try New Things and Overcome Challenges,' 22 April 2018. https://playfulnotes.com/growth-mindset-activities/.

Prada, Jenna. 'EF Skill Building.' *Smart Kids* (blog), 25 April 2022. https://www.

smartkidswithld.org/getting-help/executive-function-disorder/ef-skills-time-management/.

Rodney, Gwen. 'How to Improve Working Memory 18 Tips and Games'. Instagram, 2022. https://www.instagram.com/merakilane/.

Rouse, Matthew H. 'How Can We Help Kids with Self-Regulation?' Child Mind Institute, 6 November 2023. https://childmind.org/article/can-help-kids-self-regulation/.

Rusack, Phoebe. '50 of the Best Quotes About Education.' We Are Teachers. Last modified December 8, 2023. https://www.weareteachers.com/quotes-about-education/.

Rycroft, Elyse. 'Teach Self-Regulation Strategies with These Popular Books and Videos.' *Proud to Be Primary* (blog), 2 January 2018. https://proudtobeprimary.com/self-regulation-strategies/.

Scarsella, Jaclyn. 'The Speech Bubble: Flexible Thinking.' Macaroni KID Merrimack Valley, 8 March 2019. https://merrimackvalleyma.macaronikid.com/articles/5c82f0559fa3940385843136/the-speech-bubble-flexible-thinking.

Scully, Kris. 'Interventions for Executive Functioning Challenges: Planning.' *The Pathway 2 Success* (blog), 2 December 2018. https://www.thepathway2success.com/interventions-for-executive-functioning-challenges-planning/.

——. 'Interventions for Executive Functioning Challenges: Time Management'. *The Pathway 2 Success* (blog), 6 June 2021. https://www.thepathway2success.com/interventions-for-executive-functioning-challenges-time-management/.

Shakibaie, Sarah. 'Lack of Impulse Control in Children and What Causes It.' *Ready Kids* (blog), 31 March 2021. https://readykids.com.au/lack-of-impulse-control-and-what-causes-it/.

Sharma, Shweta. '15 Quotes Highlighting The Role Of Executive Functions.' *Number Dyslexia* (blog), 6 December 2022. https://numberdyslexia.com/executive-function-quotes/.

Sippl, Amy. 'Executive Functioning Skills 101: Flexibility'. Life Skills Advocate, 18 February 2021. https://lifeskillsadvocate.com/blog/executive-functioning-skills-101-flexibility/.

——. 'Executive Functioning Skills 101: The Basics of Planning'. Life Skills Advocate, 9 July 2020. https://lifeskillsadvocate.com/blog/executive-functioning-skills-101-the-basics-of-planning/.

Steinbach, Nancy, and Steve Ember. 'Children, Self-Control and "Executive Function"'. LD OnLine, 27 May 2008. https://www.ldonline.org/ld-topics/behavior-social-skills/children-self-control-and-executive-function.

Sumpter, Tera. 'Eight Tips for Improving Executive Functioning Through

Planning.' Tera Sumpter, 2022. https://terasumpter.com/blog/eight-tips-for-improving-executive-functioning-through-planning.

——. *The Seeds of Learning: A Cognitive Processing Model for Speech, Language, Literacy, and Executive Functioning.* ELH Publishing, 2022.

Thorne, Glenda. '10 Strategies to Enhance Students' Memory'. Reading Rockets, 2024. https://www.readingrockets.org/topics/brain-and-learning/articles/10-strategies-enhance-students-memory.

Webb, Amy. 'Executive Functioning Skills Activities for Preschoolers {that Really Are Fun!}'. The Thoughtful Parent, 17 April 2019. https://thoughtfulparent.com/inside-preschool-mind.html.

Watson, Angela. 2014.How Working Memory Games Can Improve Kids' Executive Function in 5 Minutes a Day. *Truth for Teachers*. 19. October. https://truthforteachers.com/ (accessed: 21. April 2024).

Wyant, Alicia. 'The Critical Importance of Self-Control (And How to Grow in It)'. *Cornerstone University* (blog), 27 February 2019. https://www.cornerstone.edu/blog-post/the-critical-importance-of-self-control-and-how-to-grow-in-it/.

Young, Karen. 'How to Increase Self-Control in Children - And Why It's So Important for Their Success.' Hey Sigmund, 16 September 2016. https://www.heysigmund.com/how-to-increase-self-control-in-children/.